Voicu Mihnea Simandan

THE MATRIX AND THE ALICE BOOKS

Published by Lulu Books

Copyright (c) 2010 Voicu Mihnea Simandan

Visit us on the web!
www.simandan.com

Scientific advisor: Elisabeth Walter-Echols, PhD

Editor: Declan Patrick O'Sullivan, PhD

Front cover illustration: www.yourwallpaper.com

Back cover illustration: www.alice-in-wonderland.net

ISBN: 978-0-557-25807-9

Voicu Mihnea Simandan

THE MATRIX AND THE ALICE BOOKS

Aspects of intertextuality in the motion picture *The Matrix* and the books *Alice's Adventures in Wonderland* and *Through the Looking-Glass* by Lewis Carroll

2010
Lulu Books

About the Author

Voicu Mihnea Simandan was born on May 19, 1978 in Arad, a city in western Transylvania, Romania. Ever since he was a little boy he loved to read, and later on, to write. He has published non-fiction and fiction in numerous newspapers, magazines and blogs from around the world. Mihnea has been a teacher since 2000, having taught English and Social Studies in Eastern Europe, the Middle East and Southeast Asia. He has been a member of the *Bangkok Writers Guild*, a group of English-speaking Bangkok-based writers, since 2008. His passions include traveling, aikido, and archery. He is married and lives in Bangkok, Thailand. He can be contacted at mihnea_voicu@yahoo.com or www.simandan.com.

By the same author:

Non-fiction:

> **The Spirit of Mediaeval Japan** (1999)
> **Quotes Web 555** (2009)

Fiction:

> **The Ironman. A Play** (2009)

CONTENTS

CHAPTER ONE

Introduction

Background, aims, and framework

Intertextuality is a set of relations between texts, which can include direct quotations, allusions, literary conventions, imitation, parody, and unconscious sources among others. Intertextuality also involves assumptions regarding the reader, the situation being referred to, and its context.

Literary critics have always tried to draw comparisons between the work reviewed and other works of literature. Such is the case with *The Jungle*, a novel that examines capitalism's exploitation of working men and women, written by Upton Beall Sinclair, one of the most prolific writers in the history of American letters. According to Heim (2004), "critics analyzing *The Jungle*'s literary merits often remark on the book's naturalistic elements, drawing comparisons to other novels that depict humanity as controlled or victimized by social factors." Heim goes even further and states that the novel shows elements of determinism that can be seen in the work of the French naturalistic writer Emile Zola.

Another example of the researchers' interest in intertextuality is the case study entitled "Star Wars (1977) and Intertextuality" (Roberts 2002) in a volume dedicated to one of the most vigorous and exciting areas of modern culture, science fiction, the genre to which *The Matrix* also belongs. This study provides a clear example that elements of intertextuality can be found not only in literary texts, such as novels, plays or poems, but in other forms of art, like movies. Roberts (2002: 87) argues that "It is hard to deny, certainly, that watching a film like

Star Wars as an SF fan is a process of identifying a web of allusions and quotations from SF texts…" It is important to underline the fact that Roberts realizes that science fiction fans will be able to make connections with other films, while the ordinary viewer merely enjoys the text offered on the screen. That is why the viewers' response is conditioned by the connections they can make with other movies they have viewed in the past, and these connections are one of the key ways in which film texts operate (Roberts 2002: 89).

Books published in print form are not the only source of knowledge that researchers can use. With the development of the Internet, the possibility of publishing in hypertext form has given people enormous possibilities in finding or communicating information on different topics.

While searching the Internet for papers on intertextuality, I came across a very interesting research paper that presented elements of intertextuality in Shakespeare's works (Keller 2002). The study used theories of intertextuality in order to provide the bridge to textual analysis. The discussion was focused on particular instances of Shakespearean intertextuality, repeated situations, and allusions in his poems, selected sonnets and plays, including *A Midsummer Night's Dream*, *Macbeth*, and *The Winter's Tale*.

I have also written a paper using intertextuality after having read *Jasmine Nights* by the Thai writer S.P. Somtow. While I was reading it, I realized that there were many elements of intertextuality in the novel that related back to Mark Twain's *The Adventures of Huckleberry Finn*. Despite the fact that the two novels were written more than one century apart by writers of different nationalities, I discovered they had many elements in common. Some elements identified were the language used, the themes, and the ethnic backgrounds the two novels presented. The paper concluded by stating that although *Jasmine Nights* and *The Adventures of Huckleberry Finn* focused their settings, plots, characters, and themes on different parts of the world, the language the authors used was not too different from one another. Through examples, the paper demonstrated that there are similarities in the way the authors structured their books, used their experience and educational background when writing their novels, and used figurative language in order to enrich the texts.

The examples presented above demonstrate the fact that scholars are interested in the topic of intertextuality and apply its theory to different forms of art, such as literature and film. The present book aims to find elements of intertextuality between one movie and two books.

The aim of this book is to provide answers to three research questions by applying concepts of intertextuality to three primary sources and identify, present, and explain elements of intertextuality in the three chosen texts.

The three questions are:

1) What are the main intertextual relationships between the *Alice* books and *The Matrix*?

2) Are the references to the *Alice* books in *The Matrix* used with the same meaning as in the originals, or was the meaning altered?

3) Can the *Alice* books be used as a means to better convey the message of *The Matrix*?

The three primary sources are the script of the motion picture *The Matrix* written by directors Andy and Larry Wachowski, and the books *Alice's Adventures in Wonderland* and *Through the Looking-Glass* by Lewis Carroll. Quotations and excerpts from the three primary sources will clearly show numerous elements of intertextuality woven into the three texts.

The film *The Matrix* has many fascinating elements of intertextuality which can be traced back to the text that Carroll built into the *Alice* books. It is such elements as these that this book proposes to uncover and explain, using concepts of intertextuality. I will select quotations from the three primary sources, and I will pinpoint and explain how they are interrelated.

For the sake of clarity this study will simplify Genette's (1992, 1997) subdivisions in **the following construct**:

- *Genette's intertextuality* (i.e. direct quotations and allusions used in *The Matrix* from the *Alice* books);

- *paratextuality* (i.e. illustrations and captions used in *The Matrix* from the *Alice* books);

- *architextuality* (i.e. literary conventions in *The Matrix* and *Alice* books as part of a genre or genres);

- *metatextuality* (i.e. explicit and implicit comments of *The Matrix* on the *Alice* books);

- *hypertextuality* (i.e. the elaboration of ideas from the *Alice* books in *The Matrix*).

One value of intertextual reading is that it encourages the reader personally to engage with the texts and thus to resist a passive reading of texts from cover to cover. There is never a single or correct way to read a text, since every reader brings with him/her different expectations, interests, viewpoints, and prior reading experiences.

This book has been written from the conviction that intertextuality will remain a crucial element in the attempt to understand both literature and film.

CHAPTER TWO

Intertextuality

An introduction to intertextuality

In traditional literary theory, it is assumed that when we read a work of literature we are trying to find a meaning which lies inside that work. Literary texts possess meaning, and that is why readers extract meaning from them. The process of extracting meaning from texts is called interpretation. However, in contemporary literary and cultural theory such ideas have been radically changed. It is now believed that works of literature are built from systems, codes, and traditions established by previous works of literature. Crucial to the meaning of a work of literature are also the systems, codes, and traditions of other art forms, such as films, and of culture in general.

It is claimed that the act of reading, rather than the interpretation of one work, engages the reader in discovering a network of textual relations. Tracing those relations is, in fact, interpreting the text, that is, discovering its meaning, or meanings. Reading thus becomes a process of 'touring between texts.' According to Allen (2000: 1), "Meaning becomes something which exists between a text and all the other texts to which it refers and relates, moving out from the independent text into a network of textual relations."

The word "intertextuality" derives from the Latin *intertexto*, meaning to 'mingle while weaving' (Keep *et al* 2000). The term "intertextuality" was first introduced in literary linguistics by Bulgarian-born French semiotician Julia Kristeva (1941-) in the late 1960s. In her manifesto - which includes such essays as *The Bounded Text* (Kristeva 1980: 36-63) and *Word, Dialogue, and Novel* (Kristeva 1980:

64-91) - Kristeva broke from traditional notions of the author's influences and the text's sources. She argued that all signifying systems, from table settings to poems, are constituted by the manner in which they transform earlier signifying systems. A literary work, then, is not simply the product of a single author, but of his/her relationship to other texts (both written and spoken), and to the structure of language itself.

The origins of intertextuality, like modern literary and cultural theory itself, can be traced back to 20th-century linguistics. A major role was played by the Swiss linguist Ferdinand de Saussure (1857-1913). By emphasizing the systematic features of language, he established the relational nature of meaning and texts. Another literary theorist who had a major influence on the theory of intertextuality was the Russian literary theorist and philosopher Mikhail Bakhtin (1895-1975). The founder of a school of literary criticism known as dialogism, Bakhtin emphasized the relation between an author and his work, the work and its readers, and the relation of all three to the social and historical forces that surround them (Hernadi 2004). By combining Saussurean and Baktinian theories, Kristeva produced the first enunciation of intertextual theory.

Kristeva's work was published during a transitional period in modern literary and cultural theory. This transition is described in terms of moving from structuralism to post-structuralism. Structuralists analyzed texts of all kinds, from works of literature to aspects of everyday communication. These theorists based their analysis on semiology, which is the study of signs, a movement fathered by Saussure. Post-structuralists, on the other hand, believed in the unstable nature of language and meaning, insisting that all texts have multiple meanings. The transition from structuralism to post-structuralism is characterized by the replacement of objectivity, scientific rigour, and methodological stability by an emphasis on uncertainity, indeterminancy, incommunicability, subjectivity, desire, pleasure, and play. Structuralists believed that criticism is objective, while post-structuralists argued that criticism, like literature, is inherently unstable.

Another social and literary critic and theorist who made use of intertextual theory was Roland Barthes (1915-1980). Barthes's position on intertextuality, his belief in plurality and the freedom of all readers from constraints is characteristically post-structuralist. Concerned with the role of the author in the production of meaning, he believed that literary meaning can never be fully grasped by the reader, because the intertextual nature of literary works always leads readers on to new textual relations. Authors, therefore, cannot be held responsible for the multiple meanings readers discover within literary texts. Thus, Barthes proclaimed the "death of the Author", and viewed this situation as a liberation for readers. He believed that all literary productions take place in the presence of other texts, and only through intertextuality are texts allowed to come into being:

> Any text is a new tissue of past citations. Bits of code, formulae, rhythmic models, fragments of social languages, etc., pass into the text and are redistributed within it, for there is always language before and around the text. Intertextuality, the condition of any text whatsoever, cannot, of course, be reduced to a problem of sources or influences; the intertext is a general field of anonymous formulae whose origin can scarcely ever be

located; of unconscious or automatic quotations, given without quotation marks (Barthes 1981: 39).

Thus, writing is always an iteration which is also a re-iteration, a re-writing which foregrounds the trace of the various texts in both knowing and unknowing places. It is important to note that these elements of intertextuality need not be simply "literary." One also has to take into account historical and social determinants which, themselves, transform and change literary practices. Moreover, strictly speaking, a text is constituted, only in the moment of its reading. The reader's own previous readings, experiences and position within the cultural formation also form crucial connections, and open new doors to intertextuality.

The concept of intertextuality is very flexible, in the sense that structuralist critics use it to locate and even fix literary meaning, while post-structuralists employ the term to disrupt notions of meaning. Other literary critics, such as Gérard Genette (1930-), employ intertextuality theory to argue for critical certainty, or at least for the possibility of saying definite, stable and incontrovertible things about literary texts.

Although intertextuality has inspired various critical positions, it is a term by no means exclusively related to literary works, or written communication. Intertextuality has been adapted by critics of non-literary art forms, such as painting, music, architecture, photography or even film. Through the use of intertextuality employed by other art forms, traits of society or periods of history can be captured not only in the written form, but also by using visual imagery.

Intertextuality, as a concept, has a history of different expressions, which reflect the historical situations out of which it has emerged. The purpose of this chapter is not to choose between theories of intertextuality, but rather to present their most important elements, and understand the term intertextuality in its specific historical and cultural manifestations.

To summarize, we can state that the concept of intertextuality dramatically blurs the outlines of texts, making them an "illimitable tissue of connections and associations" (Barthes 1981: 39). Of course, it entirely depends on the reader's sensibility and background knowledge to make all the necessary connections in order to get the most out of a text.

Saussure's influences on intertextuality

Contemporary literary and cultural theory is viewed as taking its origins from the birth of modern linguistics, which emerged in the work of Ferdinand de Saussure. His ideas about language structure influenced the development of the linguistic theory known as structuralism. Saussure developed a theory of language that saw it as a structured system of elements, rules, and meanings that were socially conceived. His methodology established linguistics as a subject of scientific study with broad applications, which has affected disciplines such as anthropology, history, and literary criticism. His ideas about language structure form the basis of the schools of thought known as structuralism and semiology (Cosper 2004).

In his work, Saussure raised the following question: what is a linguistic sign? He produced a definition in which a sign is imagined as a two-sided coin combining a "signified" (concept) and a "signifier" (sound-image). The notion of the linguistic sign emphasizes that its meaning is non-referential. This means that a sign is not a word's reference to some object in the world but the combination between the signifier and the signified.

Saussure imagined a new science which would study "the life of signs within society" (Saussure 1974: 16) which he called "semiology." Structuralism, a critical, philosophical, and cultural movement based on the notions of Saussurean semiology, sought from the 1950s onwards, to produce revolutionary redescriptions of human culture in terms of sign-systems. This point in the history of literary theory can be considered as one origin of the theory of intertextuality.

Semiology theories force us to reconsider the nature of literary works themselves. No longer the product of an author's original thoughts, and no longer perceived as referential in function, the literary work is viewed not as the container of meaning, but as a space in which potentially vast numbers of relations co-exist. The literary work can now be understood only in a comparative way. The reader moves outwards from the work's apparent structure into the relations it possesses with other works and other linguistic structures. Thus, even apparently realistic texts generate their meaning out of their relation to literary and cultural systems, rather than out of any direct representation of the physical world.

Bakhtin's influences on intertextuality

Mikhail Bakhtin, the founder of dialogism, has become very influential within the fields of literary theory and criticism, and in linguistics, political and social theory, philosophy and many other disciplines. In the 1960s, when Kristeva introduced the term intertextuality, Bakhtin's work was relatively unknown and much of it unpublished. One can say that Kristeva's concept of intertextuality and the work of Bakhtin cannot be separated and, to understand intertextuality, a detailed look at Bakhtin's theories is required.

Bakhtin's early writings were devoted to both ethics and aesthetics. Although he disagreed with the Russian formalists, who believed that a literary text was a crafted thing, the sum of its technical devices, at the same time he learned a great deal from the formalists. Bakhtin instead argued for the semantic aspects of literary work, saying that what mattered was not merely how a work was made, but what its meaning was. In particular, he stressed the importance of its meaning in the social and historical context.

His monograph entitled *Estetika Slovesnogo Tvorchestva* (1952-1953; *Speech Genres*, 1986), best exemplifies his theory of dialogism. His life-long insistence was that all linguistic communication occurs in specific social situations and between specific classes and groups of language-users:

> The life of the word is contained in its transfer from one mouth to another, from one context to another context, from one social collective to another, from one generation to another generation. In this process the word does not forget its own

20

path and cannot completely free itself from the power of those concrete contexts into which it has entered (Bakhtin 1984: 201).

Associating with Pavel N. Medvedev and Valentin N. Volosinov, two Russian critics, Bakhtin developed an alternative to the Saussurean theory of language discussed above. They argued that language comes into being within social situations and is thus bound-up with specific social elements. They underlined the fact that language is utilized by individuals in specific social contexts. Language, seen in its social dimension and dynamics, is constantly reflecting and transforming class, institutional, national, and group interests.

The crucial concept in their theory is "utterance," a word that reflects the human-centred and socially bound aspect of language. Language responds to previous utterances and to pre-existing patterns of meaning, but also promotes and seeks to promote further responses. Thus, Bakhtin's understanding of what Kristeva called intertextuality is that one cannot recognize an utterance or even a written work as if it were singular in meaning, unconnected to previous and future utterances or words:

> A word is a bridge thrown between myself and another. If one end of the bridge depends on me, then the other depends on my addressee. A word is territory shared by both addresser and addressee, by the speaker and his interlocutor (Bakhtin and Volosinov 1986: 95).

No utterance or word is independent. All utterances depend on, or call to, other utterances. No utterance itself is singular. All utterances are shot through with other, completing and conflicting voices (Allen 2000: 18).

Kristeva's concepts of intertextuality

For Saussure the relational nature of the word emerges from a vision of language seen as a generalized and abstract system which includes the spoken word and that which is spoken about. For Mikhail Bakhtin the relation originates from the existence of the word within specific social registers, and specific moments of utterance and reception. Since neither Saussure nor Bakhtin actually employs the term, most people credit Julia Kristeva as being the inventor of the term "intertextuality." Kristeva has been influenced by both Saussurean and Bakhtinian models and attempts to combine their major theories.

In the mid-1960s the French intellectual scene was one in which many established theories in philosophy, political theory, and psychoanalytic theory were being transformed by structuralists who had their origins in Saussurean linguistics. But there were also others who criticized Saussure's theories, and who would later on become the post-structuralists. Attention to the role of literature and literary language was crucial to the rise of post-structualist theory.

In her writings, Kristeva attacked the stable signification centered on the transformation of Saussure's concept of semiology into what was called semiotics. Structuralist semiotics argued for the objectivity of language, stating that myths, oral cultural traditions, literary texts, or any cultural text can be scientifically analyzed. But this approach neglected to give attention to the human subject who performs the utterance under consideration. It also does not account for the fact that signifiers are plural, full of historical meaning, directed not so much to stable signifiers as to a domain of other signifiers. All these aspects which were not taken into consideration by structuralist semiotics are exploited in Kristeva's work, from which emerges her theory of intertextuality.

Kristeva established a new mode of semiotics, which she calls "semianalysis." She emphasizes in this approach the idea that texts are always in a state of production, rather than being products to be quickly consumed. In her view, ideas are not presented as finished, consumable products, but are presented in such a way as to encourage readers to come up with their own interpretation of its meaning. Kristeva's new semiotics of production thus blurs the distinction between science, or the logical, and language and imagination.

Kristeva was influenced not only by Saussure's theories, but also by Bakhtin's. It is through the combination of the Saussurean and Bakhtinian theories that Kristeva's notion of intertextuality immerged. In *Desire in Language: A Semiotic Approach to Literature and Art* (1980), Kristeva revised and redirected Bakhtin's work in one of her most important essays: *The Bounded Text* (pp. 36-63) and also in *Word, Dialogue, and Novel* (pp. 64-91). In this work, she is concerned with establishing the manner in which a text is constructed of already existent discourse. She argues that authors do not create their texts from their own mind, but rather compile them from pre-existent texts. Thus, the text becomes "a permutation of texts, an intertextuality in the space of a given text," in which "several utterances, taken from other texts, intersect and neutralize one another" (Kristeva 1980: 36).

She argues that, the text is not an individual, isolated object but a compilation of cultural textuality. Kristeva believes that the individual text and the cultural text are made from the same textual material and cannot be separated from each other. This is basically a re-phrasing of the Bakhtinian notion of the "dialogue," which established a relation between author, work, reader, society, and history. The distinction is that Kristeva's theory paid close attention to text, textuality, and their relation to ideological structures. Bakhtin's work centers on human subjects using language in specific social situations, while Kristeva's work deals with more abstract notions, such as text and textuality. However, both Bakhtin and Kristeva believed that texts cannot be separated from the larger cultural or social textuality out of which they are constructed. Therefore, all texts contain ideological structures expressed through discourse.

According to Kristeva, texts do not present clear and stable meanings. They embody society's conflict over the meaning of words. Thus, intertextuality deals with a text's existence within society and history. Texts have no unity or unified meaning of their own; they are thoroughly connected to on-going cultural and social processes. A text's meaning is understood, in Kristeva's view, as a temporary re-arrangement of elements with socially pre-existent meaning. Meaning then, is simultaneously both 'inside' (reader's view) and 'outside' (society's influence) the text.

The communication between author and reader is always paired with an intertextual relation between words and their prior existence in past texts. As Kristeva stated: "any text is constructed as a mosaic of quotations; any text is the absorption and transformation of another" (Kristeva 1980: 66).

Kristeva argues that intertextuality coincides with the rise of Modernism, a period of cultural practice usually dated from the beginning of the 20th century and the publication of such authors as James Joyce, Marcel Proust, and Franz Kafka. Kristeva's work on intertextuality focuses heavily on the late 19th century and early 20th century avant-garde writing. The avant-garde writers drew their inspiration from the invention and application of new or unconventional techniques, thus breaking free from old conventions, while challenging the norms.

Kristeva's semianalytical approach extends beyond the literary text and includes other art forms, such as music, painting, and dance. It is thus not far fetched to assert that motion pictures should also be included in this category. Kristeva recognized that texts do not just utilize previous texts or other art forms but, rather, they transform them, which is why these sources are so difficult to identify.

Barthes's elements of intertextuality

The most eloquent theorist of intertextuality, who always attacked the notions of stable meaning and unquestionable truth, was Roland Barthes. He is associated with structuralism, post-structuralism, and semiotics. In his essay *Theory of the Text* (1981), Barthes defined what he meant by the term 'text' and 'intertextuality'. Barthes built his theory on both Kristeva's and Bakhtin's work.

25

A textual scholar is considered to be someone concerned with manuscript studies, with the task of determining the validity of a text. Barthes argued that not the 'text' is the material inscription of a 'work', but the 'work' is the material, offering the possibility of meaning, closure and thus of interpretation. The term 'text' is considered to be the act of writing. Barthes makes it clear that we should not confuse the text and the work: "The work is held in the hand, the text in language" (1981: 39).

Barthes's theory of text involves the theory of intertextuality because the text offers a plurality of meanings and is also woven out of numerous already existing texts. The text is not a unified, isolated object that gives a singular meaning, but an element open to various interpretations. Similar to Kristeva, Barthes considered that only literature written after the emergence of Modernism allows the reader to become fully active in the production of meaning. Only Modernist literature and the literature that follows it give examples of "texts" which can be re-interpreted, rather than just simply read, by the reader.

Barthes emphasizes the role of the reader in the production of meaning, and he distinguished two types of readers: on the one hand, "consumers" who read the work for stable meaning, and on the other hand, readers who are productive in their reading, which he called "writers of the text". The readers that engage themselves in the second kind of reading are, in Barthes words, doing "textual analysis," in contrast with the more traditional "criticism." This practice of reading, seen as re-writing, is at the basis of Barthes theory of intertextuality.

One of the most widely-known features of intertextuality is Barthes' claim of the "death of the Author" (Barthes 1977: 142-148).

Barthes combines psychoanalytical and linguistic theories to argue that the origin of the text is not a unified authorial consciousness, but a plurality of other words, other utterances, and other texts.

Therefore, Barthes suggests that the meaning of the author's words does not originate from the author's own unique consciousness, but from the place of those words within linguistic and cultural systems. The author has the role of a compiler, or arranger, of pre-existent possibilities within the language system. Each word, sentence, paragraph or whole text that the author produces takes its origins from the language system out of which it has been produced. Thus, the meanings are expressed in terms of the same system. The view of language expressed by Barthes in this way is what theorists have termed intertextual.

Intertextuality for Barthes means that nothing exists outside the text. Barthes' intertextual theory destroys the idea that meaning comes from, and is the property of, the individual author. Allen synthesizes this view by saying that "the modern scriptor, when s/he writes, is always already in a process of reading and re-writing. Meaning comes not from the author but from language viewed intertextually" (2000: 74).

The intertextual nature of writing turns both the traditional author and the traditional critic, into readers. Barthes concludes *The Death of the Author* with the following lines:

> ... a text is made from multiple writings, drawn from many cultures and entering into mutual relations of dialogue, parody, contestation, but there is one place where this multiplicity is focused, and that place is the reader, not, as hitherto said, the author. The reader is the space on which all the quotations that

make up the writing are inscribed without any of them being lost; a text's unity lies not in its origin but in its destination... the birth of the reader must be at the cost of the death of the Author (Barthes 1977: 148).

Barthes's most important discussions of textual analysis were written in the late 1960s and early 1970s, during a period in which post-structuralism was emerging from within structuralism. Thus, textual analysis is not considered as a critique of structuralism, but as a part of a new movement. Some of the most relevant examples of textual analysis produced by Barthes are based on readings of literary works. In his textual analysis, Barthes tried "to say no longer *from where* the text comes (historical criticism), nor even *how* it is made (structural analysis), but how it is unmade, how it explodes, disseminates - by what coded paths it *goes off*" (Barthes 1977: 126-127) (italics from original).

Although Saussure's, Bakhtian's, Kristeva's and Barthes's works are sources of intertextual conceptualization, they fail to develop a rigorous theory of how to use intertextuality when analyzing texts. Barthes's post-structuralist texts are examples of a radical form of intertextuality, rather than intertextual theory as it exists in critical practice. This is one reason why critics had to move away from post-structuralist theories and discover ways in which intertextuality could be applied to the analysis of other texts.

Genette's elements of intertextuality

A more limited version of intertextuality has been developed in a number of theories, starting from the late 1960s onward. A very important representative of such a trend is the contemporary French theorist and critic Gérard Genette.

Structuralists believe in criticism's ability to locate and describe a text's significance, even if that significance concerns an intertextual relation between a text and other texts. Post-structuralists reject the idea that criticism can retrace the origins of a text. Thus, intertextual theorists have been divided into two camps. The first camp, structuralist in nature, believes that the signification of a text can be fully explained by describing the basic units that form the text and their relation to other texts. The second camp, post-structuralist in nature, emphasizes the uncertainty of discovering the relation between signifier and signified.

Genette is considered to be a theorist of the first camp, who takes a structuralist approach to intertextuality. Structuralists refocus their attention away from the details of individual works to the systems out of which they have been constructed. Genette is not concerned with individual symbols or individual works, but with the way in which signs and texts function within and are generated by describable systems, codes, cultural practices, and rituals.

Genette focuses the major part of his studies on the nature of narrative discourse and especially narrative fiction. In his trilogy, composed of *The Architect: An Introduction* (1992), *Palimpsests:*

Literature in the Second Degree (1997a), and *Paratexts: Thresholds of Interpretation* (1997b), Genette produces a coherent theory and map of what he terms "transtextuality," which can be translated as a structuralist approach to intertextuality.

According to Genette, transtextuality, or textual transcendence, includes elements of imitation, transformation, and the classification of types of discourse. In his own words, transtextuality is "all that sets the text in relationship, whether obvious or concealed with other texts" (Genette 1992: 83-84). Transtextuality is basically Genette's version of intertextuality. Genette coins the term transtextuality to distance his approach from post-structural approaches. Genette uses the concept of transtextuality in such a way as to show how texts can be systematically interpreted and understood. In order to do so, Genette subdivides the term transtextuality into five more specific categories: intertextuality, paratextuality, metatextuality, hypertextuality, and architextuality.

Genette's first kind of transtextuality, perhaps a little confusing, is **intertextuality**. Genette's concept of intertextuality is reduced to "a relationship of co-presence between two texts or among several texts" and as "the actual presence of one text within another" (Genette 1992: 1-2). Genette's intertextuality consists of quotation, plagiarism, and allusion, thus providing a pragmatic and determinable intertextual relationship between specific elements of individual texts. What Genette desires is to place any specific element of textuality within a viable system that can be easily applied.

The second type of transtextuality is **paratextuality**, explored in Genette's study *Paratexts: Thresholds of Interpretation* (1997b). The

30

paratext in Genette's conception marks the elements at the entrance of the text, which help to direct and control the reception of a text by its readers. This threshold consists of a peritext and an epitext.

The peritext includes elements such as titles, chapter titles, prefaces, captions and notes. It also involves dedications, illustrations, epigraphs and prefaces which, in Genette's opinion, can have a major effect on the interpretation of a text. The epitext consists of elements outside of the text in question, such as interviews, publicity announcements, reviews by and addressed to critics, private letters, and other authorial and editorial discourse. The paratext is thus the sum of the peritext and the epitext.

The paratext performs various pragmatic functions which guide the readers to understand when the text was published, who published it, for what purpose, and how it should or should not be read.

Genette makes a distinction between paratexts, which are autographic; by the author, and allographic; by someone other than the author, such as an editor or a publisher. The main function of the autographic or allographic preface is to encourage the reader to read the text, and to instruct the reader in how to read the text properly.

With his account of paratextuality, Genette takes a different stance than the post-structuralists who dismissed the authorial intention. The structuralist version of intertextuality reasserts the importance of authorial intention.

The third type of transtextuality is **metatextuality**, which denotes explicit or implicit references of one text on another text. In Genette's own words, "it unites a given text to another, of which it speaks without necessarily citing it (without summoning it), in fact sometimes even without naming it" (Genette 1997a: 4). Genette explicitly refers to clear and obvious references that express all details in a clear and obvious way, leaving no doubt as to the intended meaning. By implicit references, Genette expects an implied reference, not stated, but understood in what is expressed.

The fourth type of transtextuality is **hypertextuality**, which is the focus of study in Genette's *Palimpsests: Literature in the Second Degree* (1997a). According to Genette, hypertextuality involves "any relationship uniting a text B (which I shall call *hypertext*) to an earlier text A (I shall, of course, call it the *hypotext*), upon which it is grafted in a manner that is not that of commentary" (Genette 1997a: 5). Thus, hypertextuality represents the relation between a text and a text or genre on which it is based but which it transforms, modifies, elaborates or extends (including parody, spoof, sequel, translation).

Genette's study also concerns the way in which a text can be transformed by ways of self-expurgation, excision, and reduction. Self-expurgation can be identified in the differences between the first serialized version and the final published edition of a novel. Excision and reduction can be identified in the works published without controversial issues originally included in the manuscript by the author.

Genette believes that all texts are hypertextual, but that sometimes the existence of a hypotext is too uncertain to be the basis for hypertextual reading. In such a case, Genette reminds the reader that a hypertext can be read either for its own individual value or in relation to its hypotext.

The fifth type of transtextuality is **architextuality**, which relates to the designation of a text as part of a genre or genres. The architextual nature of texts also includes thematic and figurative expectations about texts. Genette states that a very important factor of this type is "the reader's expectations, and thus their reception of the work" (Genette 1997a: 5).

Genette admits the fact that the five types of transtextuality cannot be absolutely separated from each other, because of their reciprocal relationship or inevitable overlapping.

Conclusion

Whether part of the structuralist or post-structuralist movements, theorists of intertextuality state that all texts are potentially plural, open to the reader's interpretations, without definite boundaries. Intertextuality is a useful tool which enables the reader to better understand texts. Since cultural debates never cease, it is possible that in the future new theories or new trends can be assimilated to the term of intertextuality.

Intertextuality can be discussed on many different levels. When analyzed closely, the choice of a specific title, a certain kind of music, or a particular way of moving a camera in films provide examples of intertextuality.

Intertextuality calls attention to the importance of prior texts, insisting that a work has the specific meaning it does because certain works have preceded it. However, according to Culler (2002), the study of intertextuality is not only the investigation of sources and influences. It includes a wider net of connections between authors, readers, society, history, and culture.

As Agger (2002) suggested, the concept of intertextuality is both indispensable and problematic. First, it is indispensable because it points to the research on the nature of the relations among texts. Second, it is problematic because it is often connected only with Kristeva's attempt to call into question concepts of the work and the author, and because its very application requires the development of subdivisions and various typologies.

CHAPTER THREE

The Matrix and

the Alice Books

The Matrix

The Matrix is considered to be "a cinematic fusion of philosophical, literary, and spiritual allusiveness" (Greydanus 2004). In 2000, the film was nominated for and won four of the prestigious Academy Awards prizes, given annually in the United States by the Academy of Motion Picture Arts and Sciences. The categories were: Best Editing; Best Effects and Visual Effects Editing; Best Effects and Visual Effects; and Best Sound. *The Matrix* also scored another 28 wins and 36 nominations from various film academies in the USA and abroad.

"Unfortunately, no one can be... told what the Matrix is... you have to see it for yourself" (Wachowski 1999), said Morpheus to Neo when the latter wanted to know what the Matrix is. Morpheus's comment applies to the movie itself, which means that the reader of this book must have to have seen the film for at least once, in order to fully understand the issues discussed here. "The Matrix is everything, it is all around us. It is the world that has been pulled over your eyes to shield you from the truth" (Wachowski 1999).

There have been previous works that suggest the issues represented in *The Matrix*. In his 1975 novel *Ignorance*, Peter Unger discussed the possibility of an evil scientist who uses computers to entrap human minds in an elaborate simulation. Hilary Putnam took this idea even further in her novel entitled *Reason, Truth, and History* (1981) by proposing that human brains had been taken out of their bodies and subsequently become suspended and preserved in vats of chemicals. Then computers created the illusion that people were still living in the world. In *Anarchy, State and Utopia* (1975) by Robert Nozick, bodies are suspended in chemicals and are controlled by a machine that feeds humans electrical signals (Cline 2004).

In addition, two short stories are reminiscent of themes explored in *The Matrix*. The first short story (Cavagna 1999) is *Wake Up to Thunder* (1973) by Dean R. Koontz, in which humans serve a machine called Thunder. The second short story (Wu 1999) is *I Have No Mouth and I Must Scream* (1967) by Harlan Ellison, which might have been the inspiration for the scene where Agent Smith makes Neo's mouth disappear.

The importance and the impact of *The Matrix* were succinctly stated in a review by Greydanus (2004):

> Love it, hate it, or ignore it, there's no getting around it: *The Matrix* phenomenon has become one of the most pervasive cultural touchstones of our day. It has been and continues to be referenced and expounded upon in university courses, philosophy books and essays, websites, everyday conversations, and even sermons and homilies.

Directed by Andy and Larry Wachowski, *The Matrix* is one of the most influential films of the sci-fi genre, with its release in 1999 opening a new era in the genre of cinematography. The story is centered on the notion that what we perceive as 'reality' is actually a computer generated interactive world, and raises the question of what 'reality' means (Yeffeth 2003: 52). After humans created AI, or Artificial Intelligence, some time in the 21st century, the machines and humans began a war, of which the machines won. During the war the humans scorched the sky, thinking that this would deprive the machines of the

37

only power source they had; i.e. the sun. However, the machines started harvesting and creating humans for the sole purpose of using them as batteries.

To keep humans under control as they harvested their energy, the machines created a computer program called the Matrix. In this program the humans live and interact with one another just like in the real world known before the human-machine war broke out. Except, the interaction is not real. The Matrix cannot control and keep track of all the thoughts and lives within it. As a result, freethinking humans, who feel that something is odd with the world they live in, become released from the Matrix by rebels. The rebels want to crack the framework that holds the Matrix in place, and free all of mankind. One such group of resistance fighters, led by their commander Morpheus, has been searching the Matrix for "the chosen one," a saviour who will free the enslaved humans and destroy the Matrix.

In order to counteract and destroy the rebels, the machines have developed "agents," shape-shifting sentinels, who are able to bend the rules of the Matrix, such as gravity, speed, sight, and strength. The purpose of these agents is to protect the Matrix and find the access codes to Zion, the last remaining free human city located close to the core of the earth, where it is still warm.

Many different locations serve as settings in *The Matrix*. The scenes that take place outside the Matrix are very strange and dark, but at the same time interesting and original (Gale 1999). The places in the Matrix have a Gothic-like atmosphere and combine different architectural styles, from modern to antique.

Morpheus thinks that he has found the saviour in the person of Mr. Thomas Anderson, a computer programmer working in a corporate cubicle, also known as Neo, an ingenious hacker who black-markets software. Although Neo is still plugged into the Matrix, he realizes that there is something wrong with the world. He is intrigued by a mysterious question, a question that surfaces repeatedly among hackers and in on-line chatrooms: "What is the Matrix?" Neo feels instinctively that this question is significant and tries to find the answer.

Morpheus, being convinced that Neo is "The One" who will be able to defeat the machines, makes contact with Neo and extracts him from the Matrix. It turns out that Neo, indeed, is the long awaited saviour, able to control the Matrix and shape it to his will. Anything is possible, one has just to awake from the dream-state which s/he has been immersed in. Thus, Neo can run up walls, jump long distances, move and react more quickly than normal, and withstand an impressive amount of physical stress.

Upon agreeing to join Morpheus by taking the "red pill," Neo is plucked from the Matrix in a spectacular rebirthing sequence that has both visual and metaphorical meanings. Neo then undergoes a series of training programs in which he is taught by Morpheus how to use his mind to bend the rules of existence within the Matrix. At the end of the film when Neo finally lets go of fear, doubt, and disbelief, he is able to see the Matrix as it really is, just a cascade of computerized digits (Davis 1999).

The *Alice* books

Alice's Adventures in Wonderland by Lewis Carroll, together with its sequel, *Through the Looking-Glass*, are two of the most puzzling books of all time, considered to be "the most popular children's classic in the English language" (Cohen 1995: xix). Both are children's fantasy books (Wells 1993) with a content and style that have often appealed as much to adult readers as to the young.

Lewis Carroll was born Charles Lutwidge Dodgson in Daresbury, Cheshire, on January 27, 1832. He was educated at Rugby and at Christ Church College, University of Oxford, and become a member of the faculty of mathematics at Oxford. He was the author of several mathematical treatises, including one called *Euclid and His Modern Rivals* (1879). The publication of the *Alice* books was followed by *Phantasmagoria and Other Poems* (1869), *The Hunting of the Snark* (1876), and a novel in two volumes, *Sylvie and Bruno* (1889-93).

Always a friend of children, particularly little girls, Carroll wrote thousands of letters to them, delightful flights of fantasy, many illustrated with little sketches. Carroll gained an additional measure of fame as an amateur photographer. Most of his camera portraits were of children in various costumes and poses, including nude studies, but he did portraits of adults too. Apparently, because his posing of children was criticized, he abandoned photography in 1880. He died at Guildford, Surrey, on January 14, 1898.

Alice's Adventures in Wonderland was published in 1865. It was written with a particular child in mind, Alice Liddell, a daughter of Henry George Liddell, Dean of Christ Church College, and had the working title *Alice's Adventures Under Ground.* As suggested by the title, it is indeed a tale of a trip beneath the normal level of existence. Alice follows a certain White Rabbit down a rabbit hole from the riverside in a dream. This alternate reality has its own internal logic. This logic is played out by now well-known characters such as the Mad Hatter, the Queen of Hearts, the Mock Turtle, the Cheshire Cat, the Caterpillar, and the March Hare whose tea parties and games have taken their place in the folklore of the real world through generations of readers. Unusual for 19th century children's literature, the story has no moral dimension to speak of, but it does preach caution and other common sense values in the choices made by Alice that take her deeper into the wonderland.

Through the Looking-Glass was published in 1872, seven years after *Alice's Adventures in Wonderland.* The same absence of a moral to drive the story and the dream like atmosphere are two of the basic elements that echo the previous book. Alice, continuing her slumber journey, walks through a mirror into the Looking-Glass House. Reality is thus twisted, and nothing can be trusted. She meets a series of characters, now familiar to most, Tweedledum, Tweedledee, and the Walrus being just a few examples. These characters have become so much part of our language that they can be found in dictionaries. Many of Carroll's words may seem like nonsense to us, but may have held more meaning for Victorians reading his books (Gardner 2000: 196). At the end of the story Alice changes the red queen into a kitten, overlapping with her real life where she had fallen asleep playing with different colored cats.

The *Alice* books, which have made the name of Lewis Carroll famous throughout the world, have been translated into many languages. On their first publication, the works, illustrated by the English cartoonist John Tenniel, became immediately popular as books for children.

The Matrix and the *Alice* books

Although many books have been written about the *Alice* books, at the time when this book was written, there was a scarcity of resources, both in written and electronic form, about *The Matrix* and the philosophy that it adheres to. Nevertheless, review writers and researchers about *The Matrix* have suggested that elements of intertextuality can be found between the *Alice* books and *The Matrix*.

Critics have mentioned in their reviews the fact that *The Matrix* uses references from the *Alice* books. Greydanus (2003) wrote that "The Wachowskis' dialogue references sources ranging from *Alice in Wonderland* to Plutarch, and is rife with double meanings." The directors themselves admitted that "Like the movie itself, there is a lot of word play, a lot of hidden other meanings, a lot of multiple meanings" (Lamm 1999a).

O'Hehir (1999) wrote that Morpheus offers Neo the two pills "With the gnostic manner of Alice's Caterpiller," and continues with the statement that "Lewis Carroll is another point of reference that gets tiresomely hammered home here."

Leo (2003) considers that the popularity of *The Matrix* "is easy to see, as it has a riveting premise, unquestionable intelligence, and a literary bent to pay homage to the *Bible* and *Alice in Wonderland*, to give the impression that there is a depth to the idea and concepts that this film only scratches the surface of."

Rea (1999) considers *The Matrix* "A cyberpunk *Alice in Wonderland* in which the rabbit hole is a coaxing cable plugged right into your cerebral cortex... *The Matrix*, with its mix of Lewis Carroll and William Gibson; Japanese anime and Chinese chopsticks; mythological allusions, and machine made illusions, offers a couple of hours of escapist fun."

Voyles (2003) writes that "The world of *Alice in Wonderland* and *The Matrix* are ideally the same," but "*Through the Looking-Glass* is much more like *The Matrix*..."

Bruce (2003) suggests that "There is a very interesting tip of the hat to *Alice in Wonderland* at the start of the film, with the use of the mirror to introduce Neo to the other world of reality."

Banks (2004) considers that "There are flashes of Buddhism and Hinduism, as well as nods to Lewis Carroll's *Alice in Wonderland* and numerous science fiction movies classics," while Forsmark (2004) asserts that the parallels to Lewis Carroll's work "are too specific to be accidental."

Johanson (1999) believes that "The film's metaphysics are... mixed with literary allusions to *Alice in Wonderland* and Kafka and everything in between," while Cavagna (1999) writes that the story is "weaving references to *Alice in Wonderland* throughout the film."

Even the writer/directors Andy and Larry Wachowski admitted that they are "big fans" of *Alice's Adventures in Wonderland*, and that "It is a brilliant book. Many of the themes we tried to echo in *The Matrix*" (Lamm 1999a). In *The Matrix*, the two stories in the *Alice* books are alluded to in many ways and on different levels. The Wachowski brothers did so because they wanted to help convey the fact that the Matrix is a lot like wonderland, surreal and with its own logical structure.

CHAPTER FOUR

Down the Rabbit Hole, the Matrix Has You

Introduction

Often our reading or understanding of a particular art form is dependent on the knowledge of other texts. In *The Matrix* there are a few explicit references to Lewis Carroll's *Alice's Adventures in Wonderland* and *Through the Looking-Glass*. However, review writers and researchers on *The Matrix* have suggested that there are many other elements of intertextuality between the *Alice* books and *The Matrix* of a less obvious nature, and I believe so too. In order to spot some of these intertextualities, the viewer/reader requires a deeper knowledge of the *Alice* books and a sharp sense of observation. This chapter discusses both the explicit references and the more obscure ones, giving evidence from primary and secondary sources, to show how a web of intertextual relationship is formed between the *Alice* books and *The Matrix*.

The analytical sections below are organized by theme clusters, as follows: The dream worlds, Down the rabbit hole, and The rite of passage. Within each cluster, sub-themes are discussed in an order which generally follows the chronology of the events of the *Alice* books and *The Matrix*, thus showing how the thematic development contributes to the meaning of the events. For each sub-theme, the type of intertextuality it correlates with is stated and discussed at the beginning of the subsection, thus plotting its position in Genette's framework. This means that each intertextuality category may be referred to more than once in the course of the analysis. For each first reference to an intertextuality category, its significance for the *Alice* books and film will be detailed. In any further occurrences of the same category, the previous mentions of the category will not be repeated.

The dream worlds

Wonderland and dreamworld

Genette's (1997a) third type of transtextuality is called **architextuality**. He argues that the architextual nature of texts includes thematic and figurative expectations about texts from the reader's part. Genette's architextuality deals with the designation of a text as part of a genre or genres. The genre is one of the categories that artistic works of all kinds can be divided into on the basis of form, style, or subject matter. For example, fantasy novels are a genre of fiction, and science fiction motion pictures are a genre of films.

The *Alice* books are fantasy, which means that they belong to a type of fiction featuring imaginary worlds and magical or supernatural events (Whiteley 2002: 163). *The Matrix* is a science fiction story, which is a film genre usually set in the future, that deals with imaginary scientific and technological developments and contact with other worlds (Dirks 2004). The readers' or viewers expectations of a particular genre is considered a very important factor in deciding which book to read or film to see (Genette 1997a: 5).

From this definition of fantasy and science-fiction, it can be noticed that the two genres have a lot in common. They both place their setting in imaginary worlds that have their own rules and peculiarities. Thus, it is not far fetched to say that a fantasy book might have many elements in common with a science-fiction film. Genres have their specific elements, and, according to Genette's architextuality concept, texts belong to the genre they were written for.

The *Alice* books and *The Matrix* are part of two very similar genres. This subsection will give evidence of how the architextuality concept can be applied to the two genres. The focus will be on the following literary conventions that are shared by both the *Alice* books and *The Matrix*: the **setting** (the wonderland and the dreamworld), **point of view**, **special rules that govern the reality** described, and the existance of **good and bad characters**.

The **setting** of a work, either a book or a film, is the place in which the events of the story take place. Both the *Alice* books and *The Matrix* have two settings. In the *Alice* books, most of Alice's adventures take place in the underground wonderland, but the beginning and the end of each *Alice* book brings the heroine back to the real world, where she is waited upon by worldly characters. In *The Matrix*, the story equally takes place in a computer generated dreamworld and in the real world, inhabited by free rebels who were disconnected from the computer's mainframe.

According to Voyles (2003) the most important part of the *Alice* books is wonderland. As the title suggests, *Alice's Adventures in Wonderland* follows Alice's adventures in this fantasy world and her search for "the loveliest garden you ever saw" (Carroll 1993: 41). Wonderland is one of the things that makes the book popular; it has grown to be its own space in our minds, a place where we all seek refuge from the harsh realities of every day life. This confusing, irrational space is what has had such an impact on readers (Voyles 2003).

The Matrix astounds not only by its action and special effects but also by its ideas. One of the most striking ideas presented in the film is that of the existence of two worlds: a real one, in which machines have taken control over humanity, and a dreamworld created by the machines to hide the cruel realities of the real world. The word "matrix" refers to a neural-interactive computer simulation created by a race of machines to occupy human minds while their bodies are being used as fuel. Thus, *The Matrix* is the dreamworld itself, a wonderland where eventually everything is possible as long as one is able to understand the fact that it is not real.

The **point of view** of a work is the perspective on events of the narrator or a particular character in a story. The way the reader/viewer experiences the wonderland in the *Alice* books and the dreamworld in *The Matrix* are different. Due to the fact that the wonderland in *Alice's Adventures in Wonderland* and *Through the Looking-Glass* is accessed through the words written by Carroll, the reader is left with a lot of room for imagination. The *Alice* books allow the readers to imagine wonderland as they see fit. Thus, wonderland exists only in the mind of its readers (Voyles 2003). *The Matrix*, on the other hand, is a film that includes groundbreaking special effects, and in this respect it leaves little detail to be imagined. The experience of dreamworld in *The Matrix* is determined by the visual images offered on the screen, but also by our understanding of the world we live in, which in the film is exactly the dreamworld, the Matrix, created by the machines.

In *Alice's Adventures in Wonderland* the reader sees only what Alice sees, so the reader experiences wonderland through Alice's eyes. The reader does not become aware until the end that in fact all of Alice's adventures in wonderland were just a dream. The books ends with Alice,

> ...lying on the bank, with her head in the lap of her sister, who was gently brushing away some dead leaves that had fluttered down from the trees upon her face.
>
> 'Wake up, Alice dear!' said her sister; 'Why, what a long sleep you've had!'
>
> 'Oh, I've had such a curious dream!' said Alice, and she told her sister, as well as she could remember them, all these strange Adventures of hers... (Carroll 1993: 141).

Of course, a mature reader would immediately realize from the first page the fact that Alice is dreaming, but we should not forget that the *Alice* books were written for an 11-year-old girl.

In *The Matrix* the dreamworld is presented from an omniscient point of view, so the viewer knows what each character does and thinks. We can see the dreamworld, but we are not blinded enough not to be able to see the real world. Nevertheless, not all the characters are allowed this luxury, and that is why Neo struggles from the very beginning to find an answer to his dilemma: "You ever have that feeling where you don't know if you're awake or still dreaming?" (Wachowski 1999).

To summarize, one may be able to say that in both works there is an ambiguity about what is real and what is not, which is brought about by the presence of varying narrative perspectives. Ultimately, readers/viewers of both works get caught up in the illusion of the dreamworld/wonderland, along with the characters – and, like the characters, must struggle to see reality for what it is in order to grasp its meaning.

The fantasy and science fiction genres are based on similar visions of reality that suspend the normal rules governing the worlds they describe and replace them with **special rules**. Both the wonderland in the *Alice* books and the dreamworld in *The Matrix* are governed by sets of rules that are supposed to be followed or are broken by the characters. In *Alice's Adventures in Wonderland* the rules are that there are no rules, or rather that there are, but they make no sense: "... we have to realize that Wonderland and the world behind the looking-glass are mysterious places where characters do not live by conventional rules... Even the laws of nature, the law of gravity for instance, do not work as they should" (Cohen 1995: 143).

Thus, while playing croquet with a pack of cards, where "the balls were live hedgehogs, the mallets live flamingos" (Carroll 1993: 104), Alice complains to the Cheshire Cat that "they don't seem to have any rules in particular; at least, if there are, nobody attends to them - and you've no idea how confusing it is all the things being alive" (Carroll 1993: 105). The same situation puzzles Alice in *Through the Looking-Glass*, where she has to "observe the Rules of Battle" between the Red Knight and the White Knight, which are just a set of nonsense:

> 'One Rule seems to be, that if one Knight hits the other, he knocks him off his horse, and if he misses, he tumbles off himself - and another Rule seems to be that they hold their clubs with their arms, as if they were Punch and Judy'...

51

Another Rule of Battle, that Alice had not noticed, seemed to be that they always fell on their heads, and the battle ended with their both falling off in this way, side by side... (Carroll 1993: 242).

Alice's every new encounter in wonderland is like a game, in that there are strange rules that Alice must learn how to master. Learning the rules is a metaphor for the adaptation every child has to make as they grow older. By mastering each challenge, Alice becomes wiser and more adaptable (Boray 2001). At first she is frustrated by the difficulties she encounters in wonderland, but she optimistically continues her pursuit of the garden (Rackin 1991: 53).

In *The Matrix*, the rules are intricate and complicated, but they can be broken. From the very beginning Neo seems to have an inclination for breaking rules. Standing in his boss's office (Mr. Rhinhart) at the software company where Neo (at that time Thomas Anderson) works, he is lectured that, "You have a problem with authority, Mr. Anderson. You believe that you are special, that somehow the rules do not apply to you" (Wachowski 1999). Later on, when Morpheus is training Neo in a sparse Japanese-style room he finds out that rules are to be broken. Morpheus tells Neo before starting the training that:

This is a sparring program, similar to the programmed reality of the Matrix. It has the same basic rules, rules like gravity. What you must learn is that these rules are no different than the rules of a computer system... some of them can be bent. Others... can be broken. Understand? (Wachowski 1999).

Also as part of his training Neo is being informed by Morpheus about agents and how to defeat them.

Morpheus: I've seen an agent punch through a concrete wall. Men have emptied entire clips at them, and hit nothing but air. Yet their strength and their speed are still based on a world built on rules. Because of that, they will never be as strong, or as fast, as you can be.

Neo: What are you trying to tell me? That I can... dodge bullets?

Morpheus: No, Neo. I'm trying to tell you, that when you're ready... you won't have to... (Wachowski 1999).

When Morpheus considers that Neo is ready to face his destiny, he takes him to the Oracle. An all-knowing, all-seeing, yet reserved background character, the Oracle prophesies the arrival of the One, who will free everyone from the Matrix and end the war between the humans and the machines. At the Oracle's house, Neo meets "a skinny bald boy sitting on the floor, holding a spoon, which sways and twists as he bends it with his mind" (Wachowski 1999). When Neo fails to bend the spoon as the boy does, the following dialogue occurs between them:

Spoon Boy: Do not try and bend the spoon... that's impossible. Instead only try to realize the truth...

Neo: What truth?

Spoon Boy: There is no spoon.

Neo: There is no spoon?

Spoon Boy: Then you will see, it is not the spoon that bends, it is only yourself (Wachowski 1999).

In other words, the boy is trying to say that Neo does not have to bend the rules, he simply has to realize that in the Matrix there are no rules, except the rules one accepts for oneself. At the end of the film, Neo threatens the machines by saying, "I'm going to show them a world without you... a world without rules and controls, without borders or boundaries. A world... where anything is possible" (Wachowski 1999).

Finally, Neo realizes that the dreamworld of the Matrix is an artificial place, built by the machines according to rules set to enslave humanity. When Neo discovers himself as being the One, he is ready to challenge and change these rules in order to free humanity from the machines' enslavement. Respectively, Alice realizes that the Queen of Hearts is just a card and cannot harm her, and thus Alice is able to dismiss the card. Thus, in both Alice's and Neo's world "normal" rules are set aside, and the characters, each in their own way, master that "other" reality they have met, among other ways, by mastering its rules.

One of the recurring similarities between the fantasy and science fiction genres is the existence of characters with special traits. Both the wonderland from the *Alice* books and the dreamworld from *The Matrix* are uncertain and full of surprises mainly caused by the **good and bad characters** that inhabit it.

The wonderland in the *Alice* books abounds with strange characters that either create or solve Alice's problems. The Queen of Hearts, a problem-maker for Alice, orders her beheading when Alice confronts her: " 'Off with her head!' the Queen shouted at the top of her voice" (Carroll 1993: 141). On the other hand, the Caterpillar is a problem-solver, helping Alice to change her shape by biting from a mushroom: "One side will make you grow taller, and the other side will make you grow shorter" (Carroll 1993: 75).

The dreamworld in *The Matrix* is also filled with strange characters that either want or do not want to help Neo. One of the most feared things in the Matrix dreamworld are the agents. Morpheus admits that "every single man or woman who has stood their ground, everyone who has fought an agent has died" (Wachowski 1999). The agents "... are the gatekeepers. They are guarding all the doors, they are holding all the keys, which means that sooner or later... someone is going to have to fight them" (Wachowski 1999). And the only one able to do it, in Morpheus's opinion, is Neo.

Not only are the wonderland and the dreamworld dangerous places (Borey 2001) filled with violent characters (Cohen 1995: 137, Kruglov 2004), the real world is too. In *Alice's Adventures in Wonderland*, right before drinking from "a little bottle" labeled "with the words 'DRINK ME' beautifully printed on it in large letters", Alice recalls the dangers that children face in the real world:

> 'No, I'll look first,' she said, 'and see whether it's marked "poison" or not'; for she had read several nice little histories about children who had got burnt, and eaten up by wild beasts and other unpleasant things, all because they *would* not remember the simple rules their friends had taught them: such as, that a red-hot poker will burn you if you hold it too long; and that if you cut your finger *very* deeply with a knife, it usually bleeds; and she had never forgotten that, if you drink much from a bottle marked 'poison,' it is almost certain to disagree with you, sooner or later (Carroll 1993: 41-42) (italics from original).

The real world in *The Matrix* is dominated by evil machines that are designed to kill the rebels. When Neo inquires during an alarm what is threatening the ship Nebuchadnezzar, Trinity and Dozer brief him:

> *Trinity*: A sentinel. Killing machine designed for one thing.
> *Dozer*: Search... and destroy (Wachowski 1999).

Thus, in both the *Alice* books and *The Matrix* the main protagonists confront evil, either as a character or in another form. They are helped by other "good" characters to overcome the evil force and come out on top in the end.

As stated in the intertextuality construct, architextuality encompasses the literary conventions in the *Alice* books and *The Matrix* as part of two different genres, but with similar basic characteristics. Although the *Alice* books are fantasy and *The Matrix* is a science-fiction film, they share the following literary conventions: the **setting** (the wonderland and the dreamworld), **point of view**, **special rules governing reality**, and the presence of **good and bad characters**.

Dream and reality

This subsection presents details in *The Matrix* as being implied comments from the *Alice* books which can be understood by what is expressed as referring to the *Alice* books. These intertextual references cover the following themes: dreams, reality, memory, and backward worlds.

Dreams are sequences of images that appear involuntarily to the mind of a sleeping person, often a mixture of real and imaginary characters, places, and events. Both the *Alice* books and *The Matrix* consciously debate what a dream is and what it is not, and both Alice and Neo are engaged in trying to understand the dream they are in.

In her study, Rooy (2004) proposes that Wonderland is not really another world, a dream, but our world seen through the eyes of a child. In *Through the Looking-Glass*, Alice gets into an argument with Tweedledum and Tweedledee, who both insist that Alice and the Wonderland are in the Red King's dream.

> 'You'd be nowhere. Why, you're only a sort of thing in his dream!'
>
> 'If that there King was to wake,' added Tweedledum, 'you'd go out - bang! - just like a candle!'
>
> 'I shouldn't!' Alice exclaimed indignantly. 'Besides, if *I'm* only a sort of thing in his dream, what are *you*, I should like to know?'
>
> 'Ditto,' said Tweedledum.
>
> 'Ditto, ditto!' cried Tweedledee.
>
> He shouted this so loud that Alice couldn't help saying, 'Hush! You'll be waking him, I'm afraid, if you make so much noise' (Carroll 1993: 201).

In *The Matrix*, Neo does not know that everything around him in the Matrix is not real. Everyone on earth is dreaming, and they do not know it because there is nobody to wake them up. After being unplugged from the Matrix, Neo finds out the truth from Morpheus: "You've been living in a dream world, Neo" (Wachowski 1999). Both Alice and Neo struggle at first with the idea that they are in a dream, but later in their story they go deeper to consider what is real.

Both of Alice's trips, one to Wonderland and the other to the Looking-Glass world, occur while she is sleeping. When Neo is in the Matrix simulated world, he is either sleeping without knowing it, or his body is induced into a sleep-like state, thus facilitating his plugging into the Matrix from the real world.

When Alice is in wonderland and Neo is in the dreamworld, everything seems real, but in fact it is not. In *Through the Looking-*

Glass, Alice argues with Tweedledum and Tweedledee that she is real, and not just a pawn in the Red King's dream.

> 'I *am* real!' said Alice, and began to cry.
>
> 'You won't make yourself a bit realler by crying,' Tweedledee remarked; 'there's nothing to cry about.'
>
> 'If I wasn't real,' Alice said - half-laughing through her tears, it all seemed so ridiculous - 'I shouldn't be able to cry.'
>
> 'I hope you don't suppose those are real tears?' Tweedledum interrupted in a tone of great contempt (Carroll 1993: 201).

The same argument is used by Morpheus in *The Matrix* when he tries to make Neo understand that the Matrix is not real by asking him, "You think that's air you're breathing now?" (Wachowski 1999). After being unplugged from the Matrix, Morpheus explains to Neo what reality is:

> *Neo*: This... this isn't real?
>
> Morpheus looks at him.
>
> *Morpheus*: What is real? How do you define real? If you're talking about what you can feel, what you can smell, what you can taste and see, then real is simply electrical signals interpreted by your brain (Wachowski 1999).

The idea of a dream within a dream and the questioning of what is real and what is not real is a recurrent theme in both the *Alice* books and *The Matrix*. It is only after the characters come to terms with their own fears and doubts about reality that they are able to use their knowledge to control the wonderland and, respectively, the dreamworld.

Another recurring theme in the *Alice* books and *The Matrix* is the character's ability or inability to remember things. Alice's and Neo's inability to retain learned information and knowledge of past events and experiences are caused by their discoveries of the wonderland and the dreamworld. In *Alice's Adventures in Wonderland*, Alice talks to herself wondering why she cannot remember who she is:

> '... I wonder if I've been changed in the night? Let me think: was I the same when I got up this morning? I almost think I can remember feeling a little different. But if I'm not the same, the next question is, Who in the world am I? Ah, *that's* the great puzzle!' And she began thinking over all the children she knew that were of the same age as herself, to see if she could have been changed for any of them (Carroll 1993: 46-47).

Later on, when Alice seeks advice from the Caterpillar she confesses, "I can't remember things as I used - and I don't keep the same size for ten minutes together!" (Carroll 1993: 71). She continuously forgets things and this only complicates her adventures in wonderland, "'A cat may look at a king,' said Alice. 'I've read that in some book, but I don't remember where'" (Carroll 1993: 106).

In *The Matrix*, the name of the company where Neo works is Metacortex. In human anatomy, the cortex is the outer layer of the human brain. In his boss's office, on the outside, window cleaners are wiping the windows clean. Stanton-Humphreys (2001) considers this a metaphor for the Matrix. He suggests that the window cleaners represent the machines that wipe away the human memory so that they do not realize that in fact they are the machines' slaves. However, in neither world is the effort to make the characters forget entirely successful. While Alice consciously raised the question of her memory lapses, Neo is able to extricate himself from the virtual world of memory control imposed by the machines.

The reality of wonderland in *Through the Looking-Glass* is questioned by the fact that Alice experiences a world that is backwards. In an absurd dialogue with the Queen, Alice tries to understand this concept:

'It's jam every *other* day: to-day isn't any *other* day, you know.'

'I don't understand you,' said Alice. 'It's dreadfully confusing!'

'That's the effect of living backward,' the Queen said kindly: 'it always makes one a little giddy at first -'

'Living backward!' Alice repeated in great astonishment. 'I never heard of such a thing!' (Carroll 1993: 207-208).

Everything in wonderland is reversed. Books are in mirror writing, and when you want to go to a certain place, you have to walk in the opposite direction. Later on in the book, Alice tries to read a book with backward script.

There was a book lying near Alice on the table, and while she sat watching the White King (for she was still a little anxious about him, and had the ink all ready to throw over him, in case he fainted again), she turned over the leaves, to find some part that she could read, 'for it's all in some language I don't know,' she said to herself.
It was like this –
·YKCOWREBBAJ
sevot yhtils eht dna ‚gillirb sawT'
:ebaw eht ni elbmig dna eryg diD
,sevogorob eht erew ysmim llA
.ebargtuo shtar emom eht dna

She puzzled over this for some time, but at last a bright thought struck her. 'Why, it's a looking-glass-book, of course! And if I hold it up to a glass, the words will go the right way again' (Carroll 1993: 166-167).

In the end, the looking-glass world turns out to be a dreamworld as well, and can also be seen as a metaphor for the adult world (Rooy 2004). In *The Matrix*, the code of the Matrix that can be viewed on the screens in the Nebuchadnezzar is made up of backward Japanese letters. The backward worlds suggest the fact that what Alice and Neo experience is not real, but a mere reflection in a mirror.

This subsection has shown examples of implicit commentary, which refers to details in *The Matrix* not stated as being from the *Alice* books, but understood by what is expressed as directly referring to the books. The implicit commentary covered the following the themes: dreams, reality, memory, and backward worlds.

Down the rabbit hole

Waking up from the dreamworld

Using Genette's classification of transtextuality, one can place any specific element of textuality within a viable system that can be easily applied. Genette's (1992) first kind of transtextuality is called **intertextuality**. Intertextuality includes both direct reference, or **quotation,** and indirect reference, which he calls **allusion.** In the first instance, **Genette** narrows the concept of intertextuality down to the actual presence of a quotation within another text.

There is only one **direct quotation** from the *Alice* books that is present in *The Matrix*, and it refers to the moment when both Alice and Neo wake up from their dreams. In *Alice's Adventures in Wonderland*, Alice is woken up by her sister under the tree where she had fallen asleep, "'Wake up, Alice Dear!' said her sister. 'Why, what a long sleep you've had!'" (Carroll 1993: 141). In *The Matrix*, the message "Wake up, Neo." appears on Neo's computer screen, then it is followed by "The Matrix has you..." (Wachowski 1999).

Figure 4.3.1.

"Wake up, Neo" (Wachowski 1999)

The word "*Searching...*" displayed on the screen of Neo's computer is a subtle allusion to the search for the truth of what the Matrix is. Neo is captured in a close-up, sleeping. But his mind is not, as is implied by the music in the headphones he is wearing. The beat of the music and the absence of any outside light creates a gloomy, oppressive atmosphere. Suddenly the screen goes blank, and the words "Wake up, Neo..." appear on the screen. And Neo obeys.

"Wake up, Neo" is a direct quotation from *Alice's Adventures in Wonderland*, signifying that it is time for Neo to wake up from the dreamworld he has been living in, just as Alice woke up from her dream in wonderland to the real world by the river bank lying on her sister's lap. The difference is that Alice woke up at the end of the book, while Neo woke up at the beginning of the film. When Neo wakes up from his dreamworld he is about to start on his journey, while Alice wakes up from her wonderland at the end of her adventures, after she has got control of wonderland and defeated the Queen of Hearts.

The White Rabbit

Genette's (1997b) second type of transtextuality is called **paratextuality,** and can be described as 'text surrounding text.' This intertextual concept includes, among others, **illustrations** and **captions**. These illustrations and captions have the role of guiding the reader or viewer into recognizing or identifying certain landmarks that the author wanted to pass on. This subsection will use the concept of paratextuality to discuss the illustrations and captions used in *The Matrix* from the *Alice* books.

Figure 4.3.2.
The White Rabbit (Carroll 1993: 37)

Alice and Neo were introduced to the wonderland and the dreamworld, respectively, by a white rabbit. The White Rabbit's illustration appears in both the *Alice* books and *The Matrix*. These illustrations are followed or foreshadowed by text or captions. The first illustration in Chapter One of *Alice's Adventures in Wonderland* is that of a white rabbit looking at his watch. The book itself starts with Alice "beginning to get very tired of sitting by her sister on the bank... when suddenly a White Rabbit with pink eyes ran close by her" (Carroll 1993: 37).

When we first meet Neo he receives instructions through his computer screen, from someone at that time unknown to the viewer, to "Follow the white rabbit..." (Wachowski 1999).

Figure 4.3.3.

"Follow the white rabbit" (Wachowski 1999)

Neo reads the message out loud. The white rabbit turns out to be a tattoo on the shoulder of Dujour, a woman who shows up at his door moments later accompanied by a man named Choi (Cavagna 1999). They lead Neo to a nightclub, where he eventually meets Trinity, who will lead him to Morpheus.

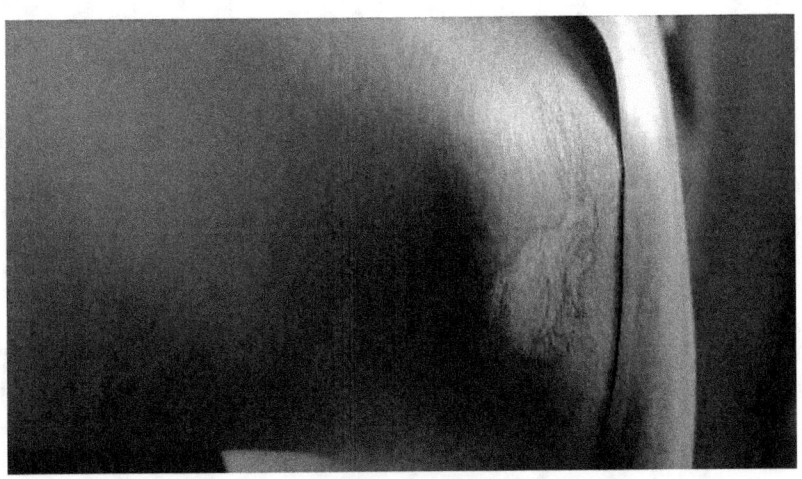

Figure 4.3.4.

The tattoo of the White Rabbit (Wachowski 1999)

The White Rabbit plays an important role in both the *Alice* books, where it shows Alice the way to wonderland, and *The Matrix*, where, in the form of a tattoo, it introduces Neo to Morpheus, and thus to the real world .

Paratextuality includes illustrations and captions used in *The Matrix* from the *Alice* books. The only recurrent image from *Alice's Adventures in Wonderland* is that of the White Rabbit who is constantly followed by Alice. Trevor Smith, one of the model makers for *The Matrix*, admits that "The script is very good reading, but as you watch the film unfolding during shooting you understand the script a lot more" (Lamm 1999b). Thus, the use of pictures and the captions that follow them are another way of conveying meanings in the film, a way that depends on the visual quality of cinema.

Alice in wonderland

Genette's (1997a) **metatextuality** denotes **explicit references** of one text on another text. By explicit references, Genette refers to clear and obvious comments that express all details in a clear and obvious way. In the case analysed here, explicit references express details in *The Matrix* from the *Alice* books. In *The Matrix*, Morpheus refers directly to Alice twice in different statements (Cavagna 1999). When Neo finally meets Morpheus, the latter asks, "I imagine that right now you're feeling a bit like Alice... tumbling down the rabbit hole?" (Wachowski 1999). This refers to Neo's sense of confusion, since he did not understand where he was going and what the Matrix was. Therefore, it is clear that the only explicit reference to the *Alice* books refers to Alice and the wonderland she traveled into.

Then Morpheus offers Neo a choice between two colored capsules, "You take the blue pill, the story ends. You wake up and believe... whatever you want to believe. You take the red pill... you stay in wonderland... and I show you just how deep the rabbit hole goes" (Wachowski 1999). Not only does Morpheus refer to both wonderland and the rabbit, but also the scene is reminiscent of how Alice is constantly given strange things to eat, such as cakes, tea, mushrooms etc., many of which have unusual effects.

Morpheus also makes explicit reference to *Alice's Adventures in Wonderland*. Alice follows the White Rabbit out of curiosity, not knowing where it is going:

> ...Alice started to her feet, for it flashed across her mind that she had never before seen a rabbit with either a waistcoat-

pocket, or a watch to take out of it, and burning with curiosity, she ran across the field after it, and fortunately was just in time to see it pop down a large rabbit-hole under the hedge (Carroll 1993: 38).

Curiosity is what initially brings both Neo and Alice into wonderland (Voyles 2003). The choice to mention Alice and her wonderland in the movie is a hint that the writers/directors of *The Matrix* wanted to suggest that the Matrix is like Alice's wonderland.

This subsection showed how the concept of metatextuality can be used to argue the presence of explicit references in *The Matrix* from the *Alice* books. There is only one such explicit reference, and that refers to Alice and the wonderland she traveled into.

Through the mirror

In addition to direct quotations, Genette's (1992) intertextuality consists of **allusion** of one text to another text. In the context of this study, allusions are references to the *Alice* books that are made indirectly, subtly suggested, or implied in *The Matrix*. Such allusions refer to two motifs that are present in both the *Alice* books and *The Matrix*, i.e. the mirror and water. What sets these motifs apart from some of the other intertextual references in the two works is their quality as complex metaphors which even attain symbolic meaning.

In *Through the Looking-Glass*, Alice again enters wonderland, but this time not down a rabbit hole, but through a mirror that magically becomes fluid-like so she can climb into it, as the title suggests. Talking to her cat, Alice says:

Let's pretend the glass has got all soft like gauze, so that we can get through. Why, it's turning into a sort of mist now, I declare! It'll be easy enough to get through (Carroll 1993: 160).

Figure 4.3.5.

Through the mirror 1 (Wachowski 1999)

In *The Matrix*, shortly after taking the red pill, Neo is taken into an adjacent room with computer terminals and other machines where Morpheus's crew is preparing him for disconnection from the Matrix. As he is about to wake up from the Matrix, Neo sees himself in a mirror. The image is cracked and distorted because the image that he sees is not really him, but rather a mental projection of his digital self in the Matrix world. Sitting on a chair, Neo watches the mirror turn to liquid. He dips his finger into it, and the liquid clings to him, covering him completely before he wakes up from the virtual reality of the Matrix. Neo has gone through the Looking-Glass (Cavagna 1999).

The Wachowski brothers mentioned, during an online interview: "The mirror is actually a mirror. When Neo sees it, it's a hallucination, but it's the direct result of the pill Morpheus has given Neo. Reflections in general are a significant theme in the film. The idea of the worlds within worlds" (Lamm 1999a). In *Through the Looking-Glass* and *The Matrix*, both Alice and Neo enter the dreamworld through a mirror, which appears normal at first but then takes on a fluid-like property.

Figure 4.3.6.

Through the mirror 2 (Wachowski 1999)

In *Alice's Adventures in Wonderland*, Alice falls down the rabbit hole in the underground dreamworld, where she becomes a giant and starts crying:

> As she said these words her foot slipped, and in another moment, splash! she was up to her chin in salt water. Her first idea was that she had somehow fallen into the sea, 'and in that case I can go back by railway,' she said to herself... However, she soon made out that she was in the pool of tears which she had wept when she was nine feet high (Carroll 1993: 48-49).

When Neo is unplugged from the Matrix he wakes up in a pod, covered with slime, with tubes coming out of his head, spine, hands and legs. He is surrounded by thousands of similar pods containing humans. A flying machine comes and disconnects Neo from these tubes and he is ejected from the pod. Interestingly, the Wachowski brothers had this to say about the meaning of the word "Matrix": "... we also like the definition, the mathematic definition of the use of the matrix, or the use of it in terms of the woman's womb" (Lamm 1999a). The pod appears to be symbolic of a woman's womb, and Neo is flushed out of his pod, as if he is being born again.

He then starts falling down a long water-slide-like-tube only to be dumped into a sluice, just as Alice fell down the rabbit hole. The ship Nebuchadnezzar flies over him, and Neo is extracted from the water by a crane coming down an opened hatch. The water may also suggest the holy water Christian children are baptized with soon after their birth (Stanton-Humphreys 2001). Entering into the wonderland for Alice and into the real world for Neo can be considered a rebirth, and thus one can say that Alice and Neo were baptized by the world they were reborn into.

This subsection used Genette's concepts of intertextuality to show how allusions, referring to the motives of mirror and water, were used in The Matrix from the Alice books motives are complex images which suggest the symbolic meaning of entering a new reality or being reborn.

The rite of passage

Alice and Neo

Genette's (1997a) fifth type of transtextuality is called **hypertextuality**. According to Genette, hypertextuality involves a relationship uniting a text to another earlier text, embedded in a manner that is not that of commentary. Thus, hypertextuality represents the relation between one text and another text or genre on which it is based but which it extends or **elaborates,** that is, analyzes in a more detailed or complex way.

Alice is the main character of two fantasy books, while Neo is the main character of a science fiction film. Up to this stage, this book has shown that there are aspects of intertextuality in *The Matrix* from the *Alice* books that refer to literary conventions, quotations, allusions, explicit and implicit references. It is thus plausible to consider that an intertextual relationship exists between the characters, as well.

The many references to the *Alice* books presented above seem to make it easier to put Alice and Neo side by side than it would otherwise be. If we compare and analyze Alice and Neo we will realize that Alice is not a very complicated character. We can observe that, although Neo's character is similar to that of Alice's in terms of the worlds they live in and the adventures they are involved in, the Wachowskis have elaborated Neo's character and abilities over those of Alice. Thus, the hypertextual elaboration presented in this subsection refers to the development of Neo's character over and beyond that of Alice's.

The world of the *Alice* books and that of *The Matrix* are similar in that both are surreal adventures in the main characters' minds; however, the stories differ in their purpose. Alice's purpose is that of any dream: it involves impossible adventures and mismatches (Voyles 2003). Nevertheless, Alice's struggle to adapt to the rules of wonderland stands as the central theme of the *Alice* books. Her determination to make sense of this new world stands as a metaphor for Alice's struggle to adapt to the rules and behaviour of adults (Boray 2001).

In *The Matrix*, Neo's purpose is clear. It is to defeat the machines, end the war, and reveal the truth about the Matrix. The viewer of *The Matrix* is also aware of the plot, Neo's journey into discovering the truth, and the climax, Neo's ability to fight and eventually defeat the agents. Although they have two different goals, Alice and Neo both engage in a rite of passage, and the theme of survival echoes through both the *Alice* books (Cohen 1995: 144) and *The Matrix*.

In *Alice's Adventures in Wonderland*, Alice is mentioned right from the very first line of the book, and she starts on her quest immediately after. Her quest is "an extended metaphor for the challenges she will face as she grows into an adult" (Borey 2001).

> Alice was beginning to get very tired of sitting by her sister on the bank, and of having nothing to do...
>
> So she was considering in her own mind (as well as she could, for the hot day made her feel very sleepy and stupid), whether

the pleasure of making a daisy-chain would be worth the trouble of getting up and picking the daisies, when suddenly a White Rabbit with pink eyes ran close by her (Carroll 1993: 37).

Similarly, in *The Matrix*, the One is mentioned in the first scene of the movie, when Trinity is spying on Neo:

Cypher: You like him, don't you? You like watching him.

Trinity: Don't be ridiculous.

Cypher: We're going to kill him, do you understand that?

Trinity: Morpheus believes he is The One (Wachowski 1999).

Both Alice and Neo are introduced to the reader and viewer from the start. Both of them are "very sleepy and stupid" (Carroll 1993: 37), but in the end they will both come out of their adventures as different people, more mature and ready to face the real world. Nevertheless, Neo's transformation is much more complete and significant, and he is much more aware of his quest.

In the *Alice* books the protagonist is not looking for answers. Alice might focus on something briefly, but then she moves on to something different. Alice never asks herself why and how all the events in the wonderland take place (Voyles 2003). In *Alice's Adventures in Wonderland*, Alice admits:

I do wonder what *can* have happened to me! When I used to read fairy-tales, I fancied that kind of thing never happened, and now here I am in the middle of one! (Carroll 1993: 61).

Alice accepts wonderland as a fairy tale, and never questions the reality of her experiences. For Alice, wonderland is just wonderland, just a dream. Nevertheless, she unwittingly finds herself on a survival course, at the end of which she emerges as a tried and tested child, ready to enter the adult life (Cohen 2005: 139).

In *The Matrix*, the focus of the whole story line is on Neo's search to understand the dreamworld. It is his desire to find out the answer to what the Matrix is that drives him throughout the movie. When Neo first meets Trinity she tells him that "It's the question that drives us, Neo. It's the question that brought you here. You know the question, just as I did..." (Wachowski 1999). At this point Neo asks, "What is the Matrix?" and Trinity answers, "The answer is out there, Neo. It's looking for you... and it will find you... if you want it to...." (Wachowski 1999). The next thing that happens is Neo waking up in the morning late for work. At this point the viewer is not really sure if the dialogue between Neo and Trinity actually happened, or if it was just a dream. Thus, in both the *Alice* books and *The Matrix* there is a quest, but while Neo is purpose-driven, Alice simply tries to adapt to and understand the rules that govern the "wonderland" of the adult world (Boray 2001).

Hypertextuality can be applied to show an elaboration of character traits from the *Alice* books in *The Matrix*. Both Alice and Neo (the One) have the will and the power to start on their quest, but they both feel uneasy just before they go through the rite of passage. Due to the nature of the dreamworld from *The Matrix* and the sacrifices Neo is asked to make for the sake of his fellow-humans, I believe that Neo is a better-shaped character than Alice. Neo's dreamworld eventually will make sense, as he is the chosen one with powers to understand and modify it, while Alice is a child with just an inkling of what awaits her in the adult world.

Double identity

As already shown, Genette's (1992) intertextuality consists of both **direct quotation** and **allusion**. Allusion refers to indirect references to one text in another text. This subsection will present allusions to the theme of double identity.

Related to the theme of 'growing up' is the theme of 'identity' (Rooy 2004). At the beginning of *Alice's Adventures in Wonderland*, Alice contemplates the fact that she has a double identity:

> ... for this curious child was very fond of pretending to be two people. 'But it's no use now,' thought poor Alice, 'to pretend to be two people! Why, there's hardly enough of me left to make *one* respectable person!' (Carroll 1999: 43).

As a child, Alice has the power of imagination and can 'recreate' herself in her mind as a different personality. When children become adults they lose this power to be just 'anything they want,' and the same is true of Alice. In the above scene, she is confronting this future loss of creative power for the first time. Alice must go forward in order to regain her power, not in her imagination only, but in reality, by learning to handle herself in the 'grown-up world.'

In *The Matrix*, after arresting Neo, Agent Smith points out that the former is actually two people, Neo and Thomas Anderson:

> It seems you have been living... two lives. In one life, you're Thomas A. Anderson, program writer for a respectable software company.... you have a social security number, you pay your taxes, and you... help your landlady carry out her garbage. The other life is lived in computers, where you go by the hacker alias 'Neo,' and are guilty of virtually every computer crime we have a law for (Wachowski 1999).

In other words, the Thomas Anderson life is the normal, everyday existence with its duties to work (at a respectable company), the government (paying taxes) and household tasks (taking out the garbage). The 'other existence,' the Neo identity, is a criminal one according to the limited values of 'normal existence.' But it is the true life of the character, which frees him from the illusion of what everyday life actually is and allows him to become the saviour of his fellow humans, or the One.

The writers/directors of *The Matrix* assert in an interview that the scene where Morpheus offered Neo the red and blue pill was created in order to underline what Agent Smith had said: "The idea of the reflection, the two Neos in Morpheus's glasses, is that this represents the two lives Neo is leading. In the left lens, we see the blue pill and Thomas Anderson, and in the right lens we see the red pill and Neo" (Lamm 1999a). Before being disconnected from the Matrix, Neo does not know that he is living in a dreamworld, and neither does Alice, until she wakes up on her sister's lap. They are just "what we call residual self-image" (Wachowski 1999) of their life in the real world. Nevertheless, both have progressed from a double to a unified identity which potentially allows them some control over their respective worlds.

This subsection has shown how Genette's intertextuality can be used to show that allusions from the *Alice* books that refer to the theme of double identity are present in *The Matrix*.

Growth into adulthood / the One

Boray (2001) and Rooy (2004) consider that Alice's growth into adulthood is the central and most obvious theme of the *Alice* books, while *The Matrix* "follows the reliable template of the 'hero's journey' from naïve innocent to hero-adept" (Greydanus 2003). By the end of the *Alice* books and *The Matrix*, both Neo and Alice are confident in their knowledge and are ready to face the real world. Both of them go through a rite of passage that changes the characters. In Neo's case, the change is drastic and far-reaching; for Alice, it represents only a first step on the way to a new stage of development. At the end of this rite of passage the reader can notice that when Alice wakes up from the wonderland, she is ready to face the challenges of adulthood (Borey 2001), while Neo, realizing that he is the One, declares open war on the machines and promises to free humankind.

In *Through the Looking-Glass*, Alice takes control of the game she is into, "'I don't like belonging to another person's dream,' she went on in a rather complaining tone: 'I've a great mind to go and wake him [the Red King], and see what happens'" (Carroll 1993: 241). In the same manner, Neo readies himself to wake up the people to the true reality:

> I know you're [the machines] out there... I can feel you now. I know that you're afraid. You're afraid of us, you're afraid of change... I don't know the future... I didn't come here to tell you how this is going to end, I came here to tell you how this is going to begin. Now, I'm going to hang up this phone, and I'm going to show these people what you don't want them to see.

I'm going to show them a world without you... a world without rules and controls, without borders or boundaries. A world... where anything is possible (Wachowski 1999).

Alice's adventures parallel the journey from childhood to adulthood, while Neo follows the pattern of a hero's quest (Greydanus 2003). Both come into numerous new situations in which adaptability is absolutely necessary for success. They show marked progress throughout the books and the film. In the beginning Alice and Neo can barely maintain enough composure to keep themselves from crying, or, respectively, going insane. By the end of the books and the movie, they are self-possessed and able to hold their own against the most baffling logic of wonderland and the Matrix (Boray 2001).

The rite of passage asks from both Alice and Neo to become aware of their surrounding world. They are simultaneously faced with making choices and are haunted by regrets. In *Alice's Adventures in Wonderland*, Alice has to face the vicious Queen of Hearts, whom everybody in wonderland fears. At first she is cautious, but then she realizes: "Why, they're only a pack of cards, after all. I needn't be afraid of them!" (Carroll 1993: 102). Alice realizes that size does not matter as much as adaptability. Her true 'growing up' comes with her adaptation to each new challenge, culminating with the dismissal of the Queen of Hearts (Boray 2001). Right before waking up on her sister's lap, Alice strongly disagrees with the Queen of Hearts and then confronts her:

'Hold your tongue!' said the Queen, turning purple.

'I won't!' said Alice.

'Off with her head!' the Queen shouted at the top of her voice. Nobody moved.

78

'Who cares for you?' said Alice, (she had grown to her full size by this time.) 'You're nothing but a pack of cards!' (Carroll 1993: 141).

Only after Alice confronts the Queen of Hearts can she free herself from the chaos of wonderland (Lim 1995). Alice wakes up, realizing that she has been dreaming and tells her sister about all of her strange adventures in wonderland. Then she runs into the house to have her tea. At this point, she has matured enough not to remain in wonderland, and wakes up into the real world, the world of adults (Rooy 2004). She has grown both in size and in her capacity for thinking independently. She has developed a sense of justice as she refuses to tolerate the unjust trial. In refusing to be bound by the unjust proceedings of the court, she comes into her own as a developing personality. Although the final moment of the dream suggests difficulty, Alice has the ability to stand up for herself (Boray 2001). During her journey in wonderland Alice gains self-confidence (Ben-Zvi 2002) and finds advancement, recognition and acceptance (Cohen 1995: 140). Her sister remains, half-dosing, pondering, herself, about Alice's adventures in wonderland and sees with the eye of her mind "how this same little sister of hers would, in the after time, be herself a grown woman" (Carroll 1993: 143).

In *The Matrix*, Neo comes from the Oracle a bit disappointed with what he had just found out, but Morpheus tries to show him the way: "Neo, sooner or later, you're going to realize, just as I did, that there's a difference between knowing the path... and walking the path..." (Wachowski 1999). Alice wakes up only when she is ready to face the real world, just as Neo has to understand that, in order to defeat the agents and end the war, he has to face his demons and take control of his own life.

During their rite of passage, Neo and Alice are asked to make their own choices. In *Alice's Adventures in Wonderland*, Alice is constantly faced with the task of choosing between different things, such as which way to go, which side of the cake to bite, which potion to drink. In *The Matrix*, Neo is repeatedly offered two options and told to make an irrevocable decision between the two (Cavagna 1999). His boss cautions him that: "The time has come to make a choice, Mr. Anderson. Either you choose to be at your desk, on time, from this day forward - or you choose to find yourself another job" (Wachowski 1999). When Thomas Anderson is brought in by the agents for interrogation, Agent Smith comments that he has been living the life of a respectable person and one of a hacker (Cavagna 1999), and tells him that "One of these lives has a future... the other does not..." (Wachowski 1999). In order to continue with his current life as Thomas Anderson, he would have to help the agents capture Morpheus, but he decides against it.

When Neo is being interviewed by the Oracle, she tells him that: "You're going to have to make a choice. In one hand, you'll have Morpheus' life... and in the other hand, you'll have your own. One of you is going to die... which one... will be up to you..." (Wachowski 1999). Neo tells Morpheus that he does not believe in fate, and all these choices create the illusion of free will. But, the Oracle correctly predicts everything that happens to him. Although Neo refuses at first to believe that he is the One, even his name, which is an anagram of 'one', foreshadows his role in the film (Cavagna 1999). All of his choices will eventually lead to the fulfillment of his prophesied fate, just as all of Alice's choices will end her journey from childhood into adulthood. Just as Neo becomes able to control the Matrix, Alice will be able to control wonderland.

As it happens to all people when faced with a challenge, both Alice and Neo think with regret about the choices they have made. But at the end of their journey, they will both feel proud of what they had achieved, no matter of the sacrifices they had made. In *Alice's Adventures in Wonderland*, Alice expresses her longing for her home and regrets ever coming down into wonderland, while at the same time being drawn to the new "curious" existence:

> 'It was much pleasanter at home,' thought poor Alice, 'when one wasn't always growing larger and smaller, and being ordered about by mice and rabbits. I almost wish I hadn't gone down that rabbit-hole - and yet - and yet - it's rather curious, you know, this sort of life!' (Carroll 1993: 61).

In *The Matrix*, Cypher confesses his regrets to Neo over getting unplugged. "You know, I know what you're thinking, because right now I'm thinking the same thing. Actually, I've been thinking it ever since I got here... Why, oh why, didn't I take... the blue pill?" (Wachowski 1999). The repeated phrase shows hesitation and the intensity of Cypher's emotions. Neither Alice nor Cypher understand the new world they have entered, and both have second thoughts about remaining there. But, while Alice tries to unlock the secret of wonderland and eventually is able to control it, just as Neo does in the end, Cypher betrays his crew members in a desperate move to be reinserted into the Matrix.

Despite an ever-changing environment and logic, both Alice and Neo continue to deal with the challenges that beset them. No prior experience in wonderland or the Matrix can teach them about what to expect in their next undertaking; nevertheless they manage to get through each encounter, ready to face new situations.

Genette's metatextuality has helped to show the presence of implicit references of *The Matrix* to the *Alice* books. These intertextual elements referred to details from *The Matrix* that are not stated in the *Alice* books, but are understood in what is expressed that they refer to the books. The following motives are good examples: growth into adulthood / the One, self-awareness, choices, and regrets.

CHAPTER FIVE

Conclusion

We have demonstrated through quotations and examples that there are numerous aspects of intertextuality in the *Alice* books and *The Matrix*. Reference has been made to thematic, character and dreamworld intertextualities.

Chapter Four: Down the Rabbit Hole, The Matrix Has You begins with an "**Introduction**" that states that there are elements of intertextuality between the *Alice* books and *The Matrix*. It also explains the organization of the analytical chapter according to themes, and the way Genette's categories of **transtextuality** interact with the themes to create some meaning.

The second section of **Chapter Four** is entitled "**The dream worlds**" and is comprised of two subsections, i.e. Wonderland and dreamworld, and Dream and reality.

The subsection entitled "**Wonderland and dreamworld**" gives examples of architextuality as proposed by Genette (1997a). Architextuality deals with the designation of a text as part of a genre or genres. In this case, the genres are fantasy and science fiction. What connects these genres are the literary conventions that all genres are based upon, such as: the setting (the wonderland and the dreamworld), point of view, the particular rules that govern reality in the worlds described, and the presence of good and bad characters. The *Alice* books and *The Matrix* are part of different genres, but have similar conventions and thus can be compared with each other.

The subsection entitled "**Dream and reality**" also showed that there are intertextual relationships between the *Alice* books and *The Matrix*. Metatextuality as part of Genette's (1997a) subtypes of transtextuality refers to both explicit and implicit references of one text on another. The examples of implicit references described in this subsection are references to the *Alice* books in terms of the themes that *The Matrix* tries to get across to its viewers. These themes are: dreams, reality, memory, and backward worlds.

The meaning of these themes is basically the same in both the *Alice* books and *The Matrix*. Both Alice and Neo live in a world of dreams they try so hard to understand. At the same time they both have difficulties in understanding what reality is. They are either made to believe or discouraged from believing that their experiences in the wonderland and dreamworld are real, thus trying to erase from their memory the existence of another, real, world, a world different from the backward world they find themselves in.

The third section of **Chapter Four** is entitled **"Down the rabbit hole"** and is comprised of the following subsections: Waking up from the dreamworld, The White Rabbit, Alice in wonderland, and Through the mirror.

The subsection entitled **"Waking up from the dreamworld"** presents Genette's (1992) subtype of intertextuality that encompasses direct quotations, and allusion. "Wake up, Neo" is a direct quotation from the *Alice* books that was used with the same meaning by the Wachowski brothers in *The Matrix*. This quotation is used at a crucial moment in the film, when Neo is about to find out that he has been living in a dreamworld, just like Alice. The message of the film is conveyed through its association with the *Alice* books, particularly Alice's experience in wonderland.

The subsection entitled **"The White Rabbit"** deals with paratextuality, the relation between a text and that which surrounds the main body of the text, such as titles, prefaces, illustrations, or captions (Genette 1997b). When first published, the *Alice* books were attractively illustrated and almost all subsequent editions had images depicting important moments from Alice's adventures.

Carroll probably carefully considered the placing of the White Rabbit's illustration at the very beginning of *Alice's Adventures in Wonderland*. Not only does this illustration foreshadow the events to come, but it also remains in the readers' minds as one of the many motives the *Alice* books are associated with.

In *The Matrix*, the White Rabbit, in the form of a tattoo on the shoulder of a minor character, is used to facilitate Neo's introduction to the real world, and the truth about the dreamworld. In the same manner, the White Rabbit in *Alice's Adventures in Wonderland* introduces Alice to the wonderland. This reference to the *Alice* books is used with the same meaning in *The Matrix*.

The illustration on Dujour's shoulder triggers the viewer's background knowledge of Alice's experiences before entering wonderland down the rabbit hole. The viewer of the film might thus imagine how Neo feels at the moment of his unplugging from the Matrix. "Alice was beginning to get very tired of sitting by her sister on the bank…" (Carroll 1993: 37) while Neo has "the feeling where you don't know if you're awake or still dreaming" (Wachowski 1999).

The intertextuality involved in the subsection entitled **"Alice in wonderland"** is an explicit reference from *Alice's Adventures in Wonderland* in the film *The Matrix*. According to Genette (1997a), explicit references are part of metatextuality. In Genette's own words, metatextuality: "unites a given text to another, of which it speaks without necessarily citing it" (1997a: 4). There is only one such explicit reference, and that refers to Alice and the wonderland she traveled into.

The Wachowski brothers tried to maintain in *The Matrix* a sense of awe and curiosity that can be noticed in the *Alice* books. If the viewer of *The Matrix* thinks of how Alice felt when she followed the White Rabbit and then jumped after him down the rabbit hole, then s/he might better understand how Neo felt when he was offered the choice of finding out what the Matrix actually is. They were both intrigued by the extraordinary events that had only recently happened in their lives. Alice saw a talking rabbit with a waistcoat and a watch, while Neo was arrested by three mysterious men that seemed to know everything about him.

The subsection entitled **"Through the mirror"** presents intertextuality in the form of allusions. Genette's (1992) first subtype of transtextuality is intertextuality, which includes among others, allusion too. The allusions used in *The Matrix* from the *Alice* books refer to two motives; the mirror and water.

The motive of the mirror as a means of passing into a different world was borrowed by the directors of *The Matrix* from *Through the Looking-Glass* by Lewis Carroll. Alice walks through a mirror into wonderland, while Neo is consumed by a fluid-like mirror only to wake up in the real world. At the entrance to the wonderland and the real world, Alice and Neo fall down a hole or tube, only to find themselves surrounded by water. Alice and Neo go through a symbolic baptism that "welcomes" them into new worlds. By using allusions to the *Alice* books, the Wachowski brothers succeed in making the message of the movie very clear, indeed; i.e. the existence of worlds within worlds and the idea of rebirth.

The fourth section of **Chapter Four** is entitled **"The rite of passage"** and is comprised of the following subsections: Alice and Neo, Double identity, and Growth in adulthood / the One.

The subsection entitled **"Alice and Neo"** showed that intertextuality exists between the *Alice* books and *The Matrix* at the level of their main characters too. Genette's (1997a) hypertextuality refers to the relation between a text and another text on which the first text is based, but which it transforms. This is the case of Alice and Neo. Both characters are similar in that they both enter a world within a world where they have life-changing experiences. Nevertheless, although Neo follows the footsteps of Alice, the directors of *The Matrix* transformed his character into a far more complex one.

Both Alice and Neo start their journey with little knowledge of what the world they have discovered is all about, but walk out of it with the ability to change and improve it.

The subsection entitled **"Double identity"** presents allusions (Genette's 1992) that refer to the theme of double identity. The references to the *Alice* books are used with the same meaning in *The Matrix*. Both Alice and Neo lead a double life, one in the dreamworld and one in the real world, and at times they have difficulty in realizing which world they live in. To better understand *The Matrix* and the two worlds Neo lives in, one just has to reverse Alice's situation. Alice's dreamworld is underground and she experiences it while asleep. Neo's dreamworld is aboveground, and he experiences it by taking the red pill that enables Morpheus's crew to wake him up from his pod. Alice and Neo live two lives, one in their dreams and one in the real world. They both have double identities.

The last subsection entitled **"Growth in adulthood / the One"** describes implicit references that allude to details from *The Matrix* not stated in the *Alice* books, such as growth into adulthood / the One, self-awareness, choices and regrets.

These thematic congruencies are straight-forward, being used with the same meaning in *The Matrix* as in the original *Alice* books. Both characters go through a rite of passage that eventually will lead them to adulthood in Alice's case, and, in the film's case, to the realization that Neo is the One, and the Matrix is not real. The message of *The Matrix* is better conveyed if the viewer has in mind the challenges Alice has to go through in her wonderland, and then juxtaposes them with what Neo faces in the movie.

The Wachowski brothers have brought together in *The Matrix* a variety of themes and ideas from the *Alice* books. They felt that there was something in them to make the viewer better connect with the worlds they were trying to portray. The writers of the script used the references to the *Alice* books by both using the same meaning and as a springboard for other interpretations.

Even though differences between *The Matrix* and the *Alice* books exist there are many striking similarities. The Wachowski brothers attribute this to the desire to convey that the Matrix is a lot like the wonderland experienced by Alice. The directors were able to take themes and motives from the *Alice* books and tightly weave them into *The Matrix*, thus creating their own wonderland, with so many touches of originality.

It is in the similarities and differences between the *Alice* and *The Matrix* references, in their interaction with the works' various themes, that the significance of the journeys or rites of passage of the two characters which emerges fully. Without studying the intertextualities in detail, as I have done in this study, the viewer of the film would undoubtedly be able to respond intuitively to the movie's message. However, this careful analysis at one area of the film's complex web of intertextuality definitely allows for the articulation of meanings that would have otherwise remained at best as inklings in the moviegoer's mind.

Glossary

The understanding of intertextuality involves knowing about not only specific subject concepts, but also about a number of intellectual movements and schools that arose in the course of the 20th century. A brief description is given here.

Avant-garde - A sector of the arts that draws its inspiration from the invention and application of new or unconventional techniques and is therefore on the vanguard or cutting edge of new styles. Participants in the creative process can be considered members of the avant-garde.

Intertextuality - A notion introduced by Julia Kristeva and associated primarily with post-structuralist theorists. Intertextuality refers to the various links in form and content which bind a text to other texts. Each text exists in relation to others. According to intertextual theory, although the debts of a text to other texts are seldom acknowledged, texts owe more to other texts than to their own makers.

Post-structuralism - A school of thought which developed after, out of, and in relation to structuralism. Post-structuralist thinkers challenged the notion that humans are autonomous and creative persons with stable, unified personalities and original ideas. Post-structuralists reject the idea of a scientific study of texts and insist that all texts have multiple meanings.

Pragmatism - A philosophical movement that has had a major impact on American culture from the late 19th century to the present.

Pragmatism calls for ideas and theories to be tested in practice, by assessing whether acting upon the idea or theory produces desirable or undesirable results.

Referential - The relationship between words and the things, actions, events, and qualities they stand for.

Russian Formalism - The Russian Formalists proposed a framework for understanding literary development which involves detailed analysis of plot structure, narrative perspective, symbolic imagery, and other literary elements.

Semiotics - The study of symbols, representation, and signs.

Structuralism - The founder of modern linguistics, Ferdinand de Saussure, was a pioneer of structuralist thinking. The primary concern of the Structuralists is with systems or structures rather than with referential meaning of text. They seek to describe the overall organization of sign systems as 'languages', and how cultures organize meaning in their written texts.

Surrealism - An artistic and literary movement that explored and celebrated the realm of dreams and the unconscious mind through the creation of visual art, poetry, and motion pictures.

References

Agger, G. (2002) Intertextuality revisited: dialogues and negotiations in media studies. *Canadian Aesthetics Journal*, vol. 4, summer 1999. <http://www.uqtr.uquebec.ca/AE/vol_4/gunhild.htm> (Last accessed November 4, 2004).

Allen, G. (2000) *Intertextuality*. London: Routledge.

Bakhtin, M.M. (1984) *Problems of Dostoevsky's Poetics*. C. Emerson (transl. and ed.), Minneapolis: University of Minnesota Press.

Bakhtin, M.M., and V.N. Volosinov (1986) *Marxism and the Philosophy of Language*. L. Matejka and I.R. Titunik (transl.). Cambridge: Harvard University Press.

Banks, J.D. (2004) *Matrix's Fun Goes Deeper Than Sleek Surface*. <http://www.hollywoodjesus.com/matrix2.htm> (Last accessed December 17, 2004).

Barthes, R. (1977) *Image - Music - Text*. Stephen Heath (transl.), London: Fontana.

Barthes, R. (1981) Theory of the Text, in R. Young (ed.). *Untying the Text*, 31-47, London: Routledge.

Ben-Zvi, P. (2002) Lewis Carroll and the search for non-being. *The Philosopher – Journal of the Philosophical Society of England*, Spring, Vol. LXXXX, No.1. <http://atschool.eduweb.co.uk/cite/staff/ philosopher/alice.htm> (Last accessed November 9, 2004).

Borey, E. (2001) *Classic Notes: Alice in Wonderland*. <http://www.gradesaver.com/ClassicNotes/Titles/wonderland> (Last accessed October 19, 2004).

Bruce, D. (2003) *The Matrix*. <http://www.hollywoodjesus.com/ matrix.htm> (Last accessed December 17, 2004).

Carroll, L. (1993) *Alice's Adventures in Wonderland* and *Through the Looking-Glass*. Hertfordshire: Wordsworth Classic.

Cavagna, C. (1999) *The Matrix*. <http://www.aboutfilm.com/movies/m/ matrix-rvw.htm> (Last accessed December 17, 2004).

Cline, A. (2004) *The Matrix: Religion vs. Philosophy*. <http://atheism.about.com/library/FAQs/religion/blrel_matrix_phil.htm> (Last accessed December 21, 2004).

Cohen, N.M. (1995) *Lewis Carroll: A Bibliography*. London: Macmillan.

Cosper, D.D. (2004) Literary Criticism. *French Literature*. Microsoft Encarta Reference Library. Microsoft Corporation. CD-ROM.

Culler, J. (2002) The pursuit of signs: "Presupposition and Intertextuality". *Visual Arts course plan*, Columbia University. <http://www.columbia.edu/itc/visualarts/r4100/inter.html> (Last accessed November 3, 2004).

Davis, N. (1999) *The Matrix*. <http://www.people.cornell.edu/pages/ nkd4/matrix.html> (Last accessed December 17, 2004).

Dirks, T. (2004) *Film Genres*. <http://www.filmsite.org/genres.html> (Last accessed December 17, 2004).

Forsmark, D. (2004) *The Matrix*. <http://www.hollywoodjesus.com/ matrix2.htm> (Last accessed December 17, 2004).

Gale, D. (1999) *The Matrix Review*. <http://www.killermovies.com/m/ thematrix/reviews/9v3.html> (Last accessed December 20, 2004).

Gardner, M. (ed.) (2000) *The Annotated Alice*. London: Penguin.

Genette, G. (1992) *The Architect: An Introduction*. Jane E. Lewin (trans.). Berkeley CA: University of California Press.

Genette, G. (1997a) *Palimpsests: Literature in the Second Degree.* Channa Newman and Claude Doubinsky (trans.). Lincoln, NB: University of Nebraska Press.

Genette, G. (1997b) *Paratexts: Thresholds of Interpretation.* Jane E. Lewin (trans.), Lincoln NE and London: University of Nebraska Press.

Greydanus, S.D. (2003) The Matrix. *Decent Films Guide.* <http://www. decentfilms.com/reviews/matrix.html> (Last accessed December 20, 2004).

Greydanus, S.D. (2004) Sculpting in Bullet Time: 'The Matrix' Trilogy Revisited. *Decent Films Guide.* <http://www.decentfilms.com/ commentary/matrix_trilogy.html> (Last accessed December 20, 2004).

Heim, J.W. (2004) *The Jungle: Literature Guides.* Microsoft Encarta Reference Library. Microsoft Corporation. CD-ROM.

Hernadi, P. (2004) *Mikhail Bakhtin.* Microsoft Encarta Reference Library. Microsoft Corporation. CD-ROM.

Johanson, M.A. (1999) Grand Unified Conspiracy Theory - The Matrix. *The Flick Filosopher.* <http://www.flickfilosopher.com/flickfilos/ archive/2q99/matrix.shtml> (Last accessed December 17, 2004).

Keep, C., T. McLaughlin, and R. Parmar (2000) *Intertextuality.* Institute of Advanced Technology in Humanities, University of Virginia. < http://jefferson.village.virginia.edu/elab/hfl0278.html> (Last accessed November 3, 2004).

Keller, R.W. (ed.) (2002) *Shakespearean Intertextualities.* University of Marburg. <http://www.staff.uni-marburg.de/~kellerw/teaching/ shakespeare/> (Last accessed November 15, 2004).

Kristeva, J. (1980) *Desire in Language: A Semiotic Approach to Literature and Art.* Leon S. Roudiez (ed.), T. Gora *et al* (trans.). New York: Columbia University Press.

Kruglov, G. (2004) *Diluted and Ineffectual Violence in the 'Alice' Book.* <http://www.geocities.com/kruglov33/al.htm> (Last accessed November 9, 2004).

Lamm, S. (ed.) (1999a) *Chat with the Wachowski Brothers.* Official web site. <http://whatisthematrix.warnerbros.com> (Last accessed January 19, 2005).

Lamm, S. (ed.) (1999b) *Model Maker.* <http://whatisthematrix. warnerbros.com> (Last accessed January 19, 2005).

Leo, V. (2003) *The Matrix Sci-Fi-Action.* <http://www.qwipster.net/ matrix.htm> (Last accessed December 22, 2004).

Lim, K.A. (1995) *Alice-Mutton: Mutton-Alice: Parodies of Protocol in Through the Looking-Glass.* <http://www.victorianweb.org/authors/ carroll/index.html> (Last accessed November 9, 2004).

O'Hehir, A. (1999) One Shrew Thing. *Salon*, April 2, 1999. <http://www.salon.com/ent/movies/reviews/1999/04/02reviewa.html> (Last accessed December 17, 2004).

Rackin, D. (1991) *Alice's Adventures in Wonderland and Through the Looking-Glass: nonsense, sense and meaning.* New York: Twayne.

Rea, S. (1999) The Matrix. *Philadelphia Inquirer.* March 31. <http://www.rogerebert.suntimes.com/apps/pbcs.dll/ article?AID=/20000101/CRITICALDEBATE/40310111> (Last accessed December 17, 2004).

Roberts, A. (2002) *Science Fiction.* London: Routledge.

Rooy, de L. (2004) *Lenny's Alice in Wonderland* <http://www.alice-in-wonderland.net> (Last accessed November 9, 2004).

Saussure, de F. (1974) *Course in General Linguistics.* Wade Baskin (transl.). Jonathan Culler (intro.), Charles Bally *et al* (eds.), London: Fontana.

Stanton-Humphreys, J. (2001) *The Matrix*. <http://www.youth.co.za/theedge/movies/mov029.asp> (Last accessed December 22, 2004).

Voyles, K. (2003) *The Influence on the Relationship of "Alice in Wonderland" and "The Matrix"*. University of South Dakota. <http://www.usd.edu/~kvoyles/alice.htm> (Last accessed September 17, 2004).

Wachowski A., and Larry Wachowski (1999) *The Matrix: Script*. Transcribed by Professor William Warner. Transcriptions Project. Department of English. University of California - Santa Barbara. Last updated April 2, 2002. <http://dc-mrg.english.ucsb.edu/WarnerTeach/E192/matrix/Matrix.script.html> (Last accessed October 12, 2004).

Wells, E. (1993) *Fantasy or Reality?* <http://www.victorianweb.org/authors/carroll/carrollov.html> (Last accessed November 9, 2004).

Whiteley, C. (2002) *The Everything Creative Writing Book*. Massachusetts: Adams Media Corporation.

Wu, F. (1999) *Movie Review of The Matrix. Seeing is believing*. <http://www.frankwu.com/matrix.html> (Last accessed December 22, 2004).

Yeffeth, G. (ed.) (2003) *Matrix: Stiinta, Filozofie si Religie*. (*Taking the Red Pill. Science, Philosophy and Religion in The Matrix*). Ana-Maria Murariu (trasl.) Bucharest: Amaltea.

Index of Authors

Index of Works

www.ingramcontent.com/pod-product-compliance
Lightning Source LLC
Chambersburg PA
CBHW060429290526
45791CB00002B/910